:k

Waterford Whispers News
2018

Gill Books

Gill Books
Hume Avenue
Park West
Dublin 12
www.gillbooks.ie

Gill Books is an imprint of M.H. Gill & Co.

© Colm Williamson 2018

978 07171 8146 9

Designed by seagulls.net
Printed by BZ Graf, Poland

Waterford Whispers News is a satirical newspaper and comedy website published by Waterford Whispers News. Waterford Whispers News uses invented names in all the stories in this book, except in cases when public figures are being satirised. Any other use of real names is accidental and coincidental.

For permission to reproduce photographs, the author and publisher gratefully acknowledge the following:

© Alamy: 5, 9T, 14B, 20, 58, 72, 73, 106, 115, 126, 128, 135; © Gage Skidmore/Flickr: 6T, 90L; © Foreign and Commonwealth Office/Flickr: 8; © Sinn Féin/Flickr: 9B, 47B; © LaggedOnUser/Flickr: 11B; © William Murphy/Flickr: 13B; © OSCE Parliamentary Assembly/Flickr: 14T; © Number 10/Flickr: 18B; © ITU Pictures/Flickr: 21; © Chatham House/Flickr: 57Y; © Northern Ireland Office/Flickr: 61B; © Steve Jurvetson/Flickr: 68; © David Shankbone/Flickr: 72L; © Anders Krusberg/Peabody Awards/Flickr: 72R2; © Gordon Correll/Flickr: 74T; © GabboT/Flickr: 75; © si.robi/Flickr: 90L2; © Greg Razzi/Flickr: 90R2; © Warwick Gastinger/Flickr: 127; © Pool/Getty Images: 10; © Anadolu Agency/Getty Images: 67; © GLYN KIRK/Getty Images: 119; © Simon Bruty/Getty Images: 121; © iStock/Getty Premium: 4, 6B, 7, 11T, 15, 16, 17T, 17B, 18T, 19, 21, 22, 23, 24T, 26, 27T, 28, 29, 30, 31, 32, 33, 34, 35, 36, 37TL, 37TR, 38T, 38B, 39, 40, 41, 42, 43T, 43B, 44, 45, 46T, 46B, 47T, 48T, 48B, 49, 50, 51T, 51B, 52, 54, 56, 57B, 58, 59, 60, 61T, 62T, 63, 64, 65B, 66, 67, 70, 71B, 76, 78B, 80T, 80B, 81, 82, 83, 84, 85, 86T, 86B, 87, 88, 89, 91, 92, 93T, 93B, 94, 95T, 95B, 96, 97T, 97B, 98, 99T, 99B, 100, 101, 102, 103, 104, 106, 107T, 107B, 108, 109, 110T, 110B, 111, 112, 114, 116, 117, 118T, 118B, 119, 122, 123B, 124, 125, 126, 127, 131, 133, 134, 136, 137, 138, 139, 140, 141, 142, 143, 144, 145, 146, 147, 148T, 148B, 149, 150, 151, 152, 153, 154; © Shutterstock: 10, 19, 24T, 24B, 27B, 34, 53, 71T, 77, 80B, 90, 105, 115, 122, 123T; © Claude TRUONG-NGOC/WikiCommons: 4; © Michael Vadon/WikiCommons: 6B; © William Murphy/WikiCommons: 12; © Annika Haas/WikiCommons: 13T; © Toglenn/WikiCommons: 65T; © Richardc39/WikiCommons: 72L2; © By Katie Chan/WikiCommons: 72R; © Gage Skidmore/WikiCommons: 78T; © Alexander Gardner/WikiCommons: 144; © WikiCommons: 51B, 135.

The author and publisher have made every effort to trace all copyright holders, but if any have been inadvertently overlooked we would be pleased to make the necessary arrangement at the first opportunity.

The paper used in this book comes from the wood pulp of managed forests. For every tree felled, at least one tree is planted, thereby renewing natural resources.

A CIP catalogue record for this book is available from the British Library.

5 4 3 2 1

ACKNOWLEDGEMENTS

I would like to thank my co-writers Karl Moylan and Gerry McBride for all their hard work, and Rory Thompson for his beautiful cover illustration. Thanks to Alan McCabe on drums. Ally Grace on bass. And a big massive huge thank you to our readers for sharing our content online and making us laugh uncontrollably at yer brilliant comments.

ABOUT THE AUTHOR

Colm Williamson created *Waterford Whispers News* in 2009 when he was unemployed. Though it began as a hobby, with Colm sharing stories with family and friends, his unique brand of topical, distinctly Irish satire quickly attracted thousands of fans. Now, *Waterford Whispers News* has over 570,000 Facebook followers, and an average of two million page views on the website every month. Colm runs *Waterford Whispers News* from his home town of Tramore in Co. Waterford.

CONTENTS

LETTER FROM THE EDITOR

I write to you, dear reader, to thank you for supporting the stellar work of our journalists this year, for without them there would be no news. Well, there would be news, but without anyone to write it down, film it, rearrange it and hide the facts in order to manipulate you into getting angry in the comments section, how would we know that the news is news-ing, as it were?

If 2018 has been proof of anything, it is that the boom is back, thank God, and boomier than ever. Some boomoligists say it will last forever, just like the Celtic Tiger did, and who are we to question them?

Conversely, 2018 has never been bustier, and not in the way that Siobhan* in accounts is. No, the bad kind of bust. The 'Wait a second, the country is still broke and we've no money for essential services' way, so it's harder than ever for the government to hide this from the general public. A pilot scheme involving giving the nation oversized gin glasses for gin cocktails has, however, provided a successful distraction.

This year had it all, in fairness, and it's not done yet. If you were a fan of scandals, boy were you in luck. Like your referendums? Take your pick! Fan of the massive ushering in of a new time in Ireland that suggests it could grow into a fairer, modern, more equal and compassionate place? Sadly, there was some of that too, yes.

It was, without a doubt, a year in which marginalised voices were given a big platform to share their stories. I hope you agree with me when I say that it's never been more important to make sure that they are silenced.

As a businessman, I can't let it go unsaid that people like myself are the backbone of this country. Without our intelligence and our big brass balls, who else would be mad enough to bulk-buy heavily discounted houses and apartments that no Irish people seem interested in owning for themselves?

For those who feel the year has been a horrible catastrophe that moved us further away from our good, traditional Catholic values: don't worry, we still have Direct Provision centres and casual racism.

Yours factually,
Declan O'Ryan

Owner of WWN, Reportchat FM, *The Irish Subservient*
and 400 other minor media companies

* Siobhan, if you're reading this, don't go running off to HR again accusing me of all sorts. A compliment is a compliment and, Christ, if you can't compliment a woman on the sterling work she does by directly drawing attention to her breasts, then the world has gone mad.

ww news

Waterford Whispers News

POLITICS

EXCLUSIVE

DEFIANT AUNG SAN SUU KYI SENDS SHEEP TO GRAZE IN ST STEPHEN'S GREEN

FOLLOWING a decision by Dublin city councillors to strip Aung San Suu Kyi of the Freedom of Dublin, over 500 Myanmar sheep were found grazing on St Stephen's Green park at 7 a.m. this morning.

The move to revoke the award given to the Myanmar leader comes after Bob Geldof handed back his Freedom of Dublin award last month in protest of her handling of violence against Rohingya Muslims in her country, the calls later echoed by fellow part-time Irishman and taxpayer, Bono from U2.

However, the defiant leader responded to yesterday's decision by availing of one of the many ancient privileges that comes with the award, including pasturage of sheep on city commons, which include College Green and St Stephen's Green.

'I arrived this morning to find hundreds of Asian sheep grazing on

the green,' park-keeper Donal Ryan told WWN. 'The place is destroyed with sheep shit and we've had to close the park as dozens have already escaped and are causing traffic chaos around the city.

'Due to border restrictions on imported animals, we've had no other option but to call in the Irish army and slaughter the foreign sheep.'

Wednesday's decision comes after more than 620,000 of Myanmar's Rohingya Muslim minority fled across the border to Bangladesh, escaping a crackdown by the army, which the refugees have said involved murder, rape and arson.

The once peace-loving San Suu Kyi later called the stripping of her Freedom of Dublin an act of war, and vowed to destroy Ireland once the army is finished with the Muslims back home.

Meanwhile, Geldof, who was knighted in 1986 by ethnic-cleansing enthusiasts the British monarchy, has suggested to Dublin City Council to ask him if he wants his award back, stating that he 'wouldn't promise anything, but it would be a nice gesture all the same.'

Did You Know?

Let it go Dave, it's been five years, Jessica didn't love you then and doesn't love you now.

BREAKING NEWS

'WE'RE MAKING A RIGHT FUCKING BALLS OF THIS'

BRITISH Prime Minister Theresa May has shocked her political peers in a rare outburst this morning, which forced the House of Commons speaker to suspend proceedings for the time being.

Flanked by Brexit minister David Davis, Ms May took to the podium before taking a deep breath and admitting things were not going the UK's way.

'Right Honourable … whatever,' a dishevelled May began, before crumpling up her reading material and throwing it over her left shoulder and hitting Mr Davis in the forehead. 'We're making a right fucking balls of this,' she said to a round of collective gasps from the House. 'We have no fucking idea what we're doing and the further we go with this Brexit mess, the worse it's getting and I just can't even.'

At this point, House of Commons speaker John Bercow attempted to interrupt the prime minister to call order, but was swiftly shut down.

'I'm not fucking finished, John!' May barked, the House now silent with disbelief. 'The whole world is laughing at us and seems to be enjoying it, even the spud-munching Paddies are joining in. This fucking shit show I've inherited and run into the ground is going to ruin everything. We might as well all jump on board the red Brexit bus and drive the fucking thing off the cliffs of Dover, because no one here seems to know whether we want a shit or a haircut,' she said before turning to her bench and stating she was going home to bed 'for a good cry'.

Sources at Number 10 confirmed the British PM has in fact locked herself in her room with a note outside stating that she's 'not coming out until everyone stops laughing at the UK'.

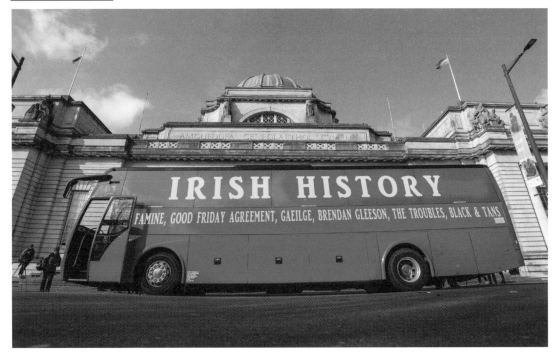

IRISH HISTORY

FAMINE, GOOD FRIDAY AGREEMENT, GAEILGE, BRENDAN GLEESON, THE TROUBLES, BLACK & TANS

IRISH HISTORY TO BE WRITTEN ON SIDE OF A BUS FOR BRITISH PEOPLE

SEEKING a long-term solution to the never-ending parade of ignorance a portion of the British public seem perfectly happy to show off when it comes to Ireland, Irish history, and the border between Ireland and Northern Ireland, the people of Ireland have hit upon a clever idea.

In recent weeks, a number of pro-Brexit politicians, journalists, members of the public and incomprehensible cat ladies from Britain have publicly and proudly declared their complete lack of knowledge of their nearest neighbours, Ireland, forcing those living in the country not actually known as 'Southern Ireland' to hire a bus.

'Recent history has shown us that the majority of Britons will believe anything that's written on the side of a bus, which will come in handy when we simply lay out the factual aspects of Ireland's history,' explained an Irish

'Recent history has shown us that the majority of Britons will believe anything that's written on the side of a bus'

person heading up the initiative, who incidentally is not called 'Paddy'.

'Unfortunately, given the detailed nature of a country's history, as many as 7,000 buses will be used as part of the education effort, but given time we hope Britain can learn its own role in Irish history, and fingers crossed it could even become aware of Northern Ireland, its border and how that whole thing came to pass,' the Irish person added.

Some buses will prove hard for many Britons to understand, such as those featuring details about the Famine, the Black and Tans, and British state collusion in aiding and abetting Loyalist terrorist activity and murder in Northern Ireland, meaning a need for the font to be enlarged slightly.

While some Britons may protest about being tarnished with the same relentlessly ignorant brush due to the fact they are from Scotland and Wales or are just not thick, it has been observed that Ireland has patiently waited over 800 years for Britain to study for its Irish history test.

'You know the way London is in Scotland, and how we saved Hull from the Vampire Invasion of 1764, and when Ireland's very own Adele won loads of Grammys … see? It's fucking annoying when people talk about something they've no fucking clue about,' concluded the Irish person.

AMERICA

PENCE SPENDS ENTIRE MEETING WITH TAOISEACH THINKING ABOUT KISSING HIM

US Vice President and ardent bigot, Mike Pence, has spent the entirety of his behind-closed-doors meeting with Irish leader Leo Varadkar contemplating what it would be like to place his mouth on the soft, supple lips of the 39-year-old Irishman.

'Don't think about kissing him, don't think about kissing him,' ran the internal monologue in Pence's head as he engaged in polite small talk with the openly gay leader of Ireland, before confirming to himself it was a good idea he banned media from attending and reporting on

the meeting with the broad-shouldered, classically handsome Irish hunk.

'But what would it be like to touch a penis that wasn't mine,' Pence's head added, contorting his soul into a shape that made him feel all sorts of odd, but very familiar feelings, like planting a kiss on the lips of the Irish leader he was currently locking eyes with.

The meeting, which was meant to be a straight-forward and perfunctory discussion which allowed both the Irish and American political class to pretend there is a sustained and special connection

between the two nations, became continuously derailed by the US vice president's predilection for sinful thoughts.

'Fuck, that accent gets me every time,' Pence added as he gripped the arms of his chair tighter and tighter

with each and every word the tall, slim and intelligent Irish leader said, reminding Pence of Cary Grant and a time when men were men.

At the end of the meeting, which was heralded as a warm and successful chat, Pence gifted Taoiseach Varadkar a copy of the Old Testament with all the bits about how he is an abomination helpfully highlighted, as well as presenting him with a gift voucher for a gay conversion therapy programme.

The taoiseach had previously assured the media that while it has been said Pence is openly hostile and bigoted when it comes to the LGBTQ community, he definitely doesn't believe in gay conversion therapy so that's kind of cool.

APATHY VOTED IRISH ELECTORATE'S FAVOURITE PASTIME

DESPITE occasionally mobilising to protest against paying for water or campaigning in the weeks leading up to a referendum, it can be revealed that the Irish electorate's favourite pastime is apathy.

A poll conducted by Irish Political Trends revealed that while a minority of the electorate organises itself into groups with the aim of pressuring the government and its opposition into making policy decisions that can help Irish society, it turns out the vast majority of the electorate aren't all that fussed.

Citing reasons such as, 'Ah, they're all the same,' 'I'm doing alright money wise, so who cares about anyone else,' and 'Someone should do something about it, as long as that someone isn't me,' a majority of poll

respondents confirmed that as members of the electorate they were incredibly apathetic.

'Don't get me wrong, I don't like homelessness, terribly administered state projects which go over budget and under-deliver,

corruption in the guards, tracker mortgage scandals, but I draw the line at being

asked to become directly involved in being part of any solution,' remarked one voter and poll respondent, Cormac Mannigan.

'Don't be asking me to send off letters or go to protests, or to even read up on issues. I have my weekends and my evenings free and if you try to get me to do something, I'll be honest, I could get violent,' added Mannigan, who was pretty annoyed we spotted him in the street to ask even a few questions.

In a separate poll, 100 per cent of people classed themselves as 'political activists' after signing an online petition once.

HEALTH

KID PLAYING 'DOCTORS AND NURSES' COLLAPSES AFTER 19-HOUR SHIFT

A WATERFORD child is being treated for exhaustion and stress after a game of 'doctors and nurses' became a little bit too realistic, resulting in a 19-hour shift in dangerously underfunded, poorly equipped conditions.

Mikey Brennan, 4, had been playing dress-up with his friends at creche early yesterday morning, opting to dress as a junior doctor because he thought it would be fun to pretend to make the stuffed toy 'patients' feel better, healing their boo-boos and making them good as new again.

However, it appears that Brennan did not take into account the pressure-cooker atmosphere of the working hospital environment in Ireland today, and was forced to remain at his post tending to a never-ending stream of ill teddy bears all through little break, garden time, and right past home time when all his pals left with their mummies and daddies while he tried desperately to stem the flow of stuffing out of the side of a toy elephant.

Finally finishing his workload after midnight last night, Brennan arrived home, ate a Cheesestring, then collapsed in a heap on the sitting room floor out of sheer exhaustion.

'The shift yesterday only lasted 19 hours because it was a make-believe playtime thing. If that was a real shift, he'd still be there right now,' said Dr Pavel O'Neill, who treated young Brennan for an acute case of reality.

'Maybe he wants to take a leaf out of real junior doctors' books, stick it out here in Ireland until trained, and then bugger off to England or wherever, where you can get better pay, better conditions, better hours. Or, alternatively, you could wait for the government to loosen the purse strings and funnel some cash into the HSE, but I think playtime will be well and truly over by the time that happens.'

Brennan's classmates who dressed up as policemen and firefighters fared no better, with those who dressed as cops being forced to stay silent on serious breaches of procedure, and those who dressed as firefighters getting pelted with Lego as they attended bogus 999 calls.

Summer on the 39
Memoirs of an undercover Spanish student

Chapter One:
It is the day that I have been training for since the Ministerio de Fomento – our ministry of public works and transport – approached me last year. Juan, they asked me, how would you like to be more than just a filing clerk? How would you like to do something that would really help the people of Spain enjoy a better, more sophisticated public transport system? Of course, I said yes straight away. But why me, I asked. They told me it was because I was being given a very special mission, just because I was the youngest-looking man in the department. I was to go undercover as a Spanish student on an exchange to Ireland, and learn as much as I could of their public transport. Like *21 Jump Street*, but with buses and something they call a DART. For this mission, I have been training for 12 months. Today, they gave me my uniform – a black sweatshirt and black skinny jeans, as well as my backpack, which I felt was much too big but they assured me was just the right size. Then they told me to shave my moustache, but not all of it. To Ireland I go!

BREXIT

BREXIT NEGOTIATIONS PROGRESS SIGNIFICANTLY AS BORIS HAS MOUTH SEWN SHUT

THE EU has heralded the progress made in Brexit negotiations in the hours following Britain's decision to sew Foreign Secretary Boris Johnson's mouth shut, limiting his ability to broadcast ridiculous statements.

'We cannot overstate the progress that has been made. Truly, this is a watershed moment in the negotiations,' confirmed the EU's lead negotiator Michel Barnier after a brief 60-minute meeting with Britain's negotiating team which was void of

> **'We cannot overstate the progress that has been made. Truly, this is a watershed moment in the negotiations'**

Boris Johnson's utterances for the first time.

Free from having to deal with Johnson suggesting passage between the border shared by Ireland and Northern Ireland would be easier than Angela Merkel after a night at Ockoberfest, Brexit talks were able to helpfully deal with substantive issues and not broad, confusing and contradictory statements.

'Can you hear that? That's the sound of fucking silence,' an exhausted-looking Theresa May declared with relief.

Pro-May Tories have welcomed the development, as it frees up the prime minister to be pummelled in negotiations by the EU without having to respond to the media when Johnson says something like, 'Afghanistan is only good for heroin,' or 'Moroccan prostitutes are absolutely rubbish.'

'Well, if there's anything we know about the French it's that they give up, and the Irish get confused when a drink is put in front of them, and those Germans are a dour bunch, just don't leave Poland unattended or they'll nick it again,' Johnson said as the final stitches were sewn through his lips earlier today, with the Tory MP seemingly of the belief that his harmless and jolly buffoon routine could actually be the source of future economic prosperity in Britain, post-Brexit.

Johnson's hands were also tied to a chair in a bid to limit his ability to write anything stupid on the side of a bus.

Did You Know?

When you die Google and Facebook are going to charge your loved ones money in exchange for seeing all the filthy and horrible things you were typing and looking up online.

DUP MARK 20TH ANNIVERSARY OF NOT SUPPORTING GOOD FRIDAY AGREEMENT

ON this the 20th anniversary of the signing of the Good Friday Agreement, which ushered in peace in Northern Ireland, commemorations will take place in Belfast to mark the momentous achievement. Elsewhere, alternative commemorations are being observed by the DUP, who continue to celebrate the anniversary of not supporting the agreement in any shape or form.

Arlene Foster led the commemorations by steadfastly standing with her arms crossed and looking sullen, while pointing out her party maintains a desire to have

Northern Ireland's affairs run from Westminster as the DUP aren't much up for running things with Sinn Féin in Stormont.

While there will be much acknowledgement of the work of John Hume and David Trimble, and the awarding of the 1998 Nobel Peace Prize to the men, the DUP have instead opted to celebrate not voting for the Good Friday Agreement by having some sugar-free, flavourless cake

before waving miniature Union Jacks.

'Some people might be delighted that 20 years ago a peaceful and possibly prosperous future was signed off on for the generations to come, but we're just going to watch a DVD box set of the Queen's speeches on repeat and talk about how great Brexit is,' a DUP aide close to Foster revealed.

Elsewhere, Sinn Féin have spent the previous week replacing every mention of the SDLP and John Hume in the Wikipedia entry on the Good Friday Agreement with 'Sinn Féin' and 'Gerry Adams', in a bid to rewrite history.

HORNY LITTLE MINX MCDONALD SLAMS SEXIST ARTICLE

SULTRY Sinn Féin siren and lady politician Mary 'Swit Swoo' McDonald has playfully admonished a seemingly sexist article which referred to her womanly ability to be a woman in the crazy man's world of politics.

Dominated by non-sexy woman bodies otherwise known as men, the field of politics requires that female politicians have a certain quality, according to some, in order to survive – and that quality, as you well know, is raw, untamed sex appeal and nothing else.

While McDonald likely outlined why she found the article to misrepresent why she was elected leader of Sinn Féin, we could barely hear a word as we were so transfixed on her libidinous lips as they motioned up and down, delivering what we believe to be a right old

tongue lashing. We need to lie down.

Could McDonald really be taoiseach material? And could she do it in a leather catsuit just for us? Pertinent political questions that only McDonald, who we can reasonably presume is a right horny minx, can answer.

McDonald, who possesses the same sex appeal as Sharon Stone did in that movie about how sexy Sharon Stone could be, went on to talk about a series of pressing political issues, but all we could think about was pressing our political issues right up

against her, if you catch our drift. And if you don't: sex!

The Sinn Féin TD has recently helped her party grow engorged in the polls, with the phallus of voter approval rising and rising,

due in no small part to her enviably curved frontal lobes, sparking concern among rival parties that McDonald may be too politically capable, in a sexy way.

NEW ZEALAND

PRESIDENT HIGGINS VISITS ANCESTRAL HOMEPLACE

THERE were emotional scenes in New Zealand today after Irish President Michael D Higgins visited his ancestral home of Hobbiton, located on the north island of the country.

Higgins took time out of his presidential tour to visit the hills and valleys of his forefathers, with eyewitnesses claiming that the visit was full of emotion as the president learned about the history of his people.

After the natives of Hobbiton presented him with a cask of ale, a pipe full of dubious tobacco and a mysterious envelope containing a magical ring, Higgins took part in some traditional Hobbiton activities, such as drinking ale, smoking dubious tobacco, and performing incredible vanishing tricks with the help of the magical ring.

'We let him know that he will always be welcome here,' said Edie Sackville-Higgins, a distant relative of the president.

'The Higginses left these lands hundreds of years ago, and they

> ### 'The Higginses left these lands hundreds of years ago, and they really seem to have done very well for themselves'

really seem to have done very well for themselves. We're delighted that Michael took time out of his busy schedule to come and visit us, and we hope that he agrees to help us rid these lands from the treacherous evil that spreads from the east, threatening to blanket this world in darkness for an eternity.'

Following his adventures in Hobbiton, Higgins will embark on a journey to defeat a dragon sleeping inside a mountain, although this trip will not be half as entertaining or popular.

Ireland's Litter Problem:
– In a bid to stop the trend of people driving down country lanes and dumping their rubbish into fields, WWN proposes placing land mines in random locations to act as a deterrent.
– Introduce a new pink bin which the public is allowed to just fuck any old shite into.
– Invent a new type of chewing gum which self-destructs ten seconds after being thrown on the ground.
– In a bid to get the public on side and view recycling in a new and positive manner, WWN suggests the creation of a new semi-state body called Irish Rubbish which will charge the public even more money to dispose of its waste. There is no way this will backfire.
– The minister for the environment should write to every supermarket to ask about why the majority of the fucking plastic they use comes with a shiny 'not recyclable' sign on it.
– It's so important for future generations to engage with the idea of recycling, so WWN proposes a new VHS videotape is sent to every school in Ireland. The video will contain on it a super cool rap about how recycling is 'ace' and 'totally awesome' and will feature people Irish kids these days look up to like Marty Morrissey, George Hook, Pat Kenny, Twink and Daniel O'Donnell. Give the key line of 'Don't be a fool, recycling is cool' to Pat Kenny.
– Environmentally conscious beheadings for people who dump their old fridges on the side of the road. Extreme, yes, but don't worry, their heads will be placed in compost bins.
– Click on rubbish. Drag to recycling bin. Simple.

HEADLESS CHICKEN PUT IN CHARGE OF GOVERNMENT'S HOMELESS STRATEGY

IN a bid to vastly improve the thinking around solutions to the homelessness crisis, the Department of No Housing has appointed a headless chicken to the position of Chief Solutions Strategist.

'It's no secret that we haven't the slightest inkling as to how to solve this issue, so after some honest dialogue amongst ourselves, we knew we had to hire someone with superior skills and experience,' explained one cabinet minister.

The recruitment drive took in a high number of rural chicken farms, with no stone left unturned when it came to finding the perfect headless chicken.

'We're fairly confident, as the public should be, that we now have an individual in place that knows a lot more than us, and hopefully this headless chicken has the sort of blue sky thinking that evades us,' added the minister.

It is thought the first task the headless chicken will undertake is working out how many homeless people there are on the streets, and how to best help them become not homeless.

'Jesus, see, this is what we're talking about. We hadn't even thought of that. This lad is going to be a huge success,' the minister concluded before spending ten minutes pushing a door marked with a 'Pull' sign.

[VICTIM'S NAME HERE] SHOT DEAD IN [PART OF DUBLIN HERE]

A MAN was shot dead in a gang-related attack in the [north/south] inner city at around [enter approximate time here], WWN can confirm.

[Victim's name here] was shot up to [number of gunshot wounds] by a gunman, who witnesses in the area said was dressed in [vague description of man in dark clothing], before escaping on foot.

The father of [enter number of children] was [well known to gardaí/a victim of mistaken identity] and was taken to the [hospital name], but was pronounced dead a short time later.

'[Insert meaningless statement issued by opportunistic politician here]' said [opportunistic politician name]. '[Insert whatever promise the politician makes here.]'

A [type of burnt-out vehicle] believed to have been used in the murder was later found in a nearby lane.

[Insert compulsory sentence about gardaí opening up an investigation.]

It is understood the murder is part of an ongoing [name of gangland feud] that has so far taken [number of deaths so far] over the past [insert number of years the feud has been allowed to go on for by the state, while making sure not to mention the lack of garda resources being the main problem, or drug prohibition].

Gardaí have asked any eyewitnesses to come forward with any information and to contact Store Street Garda Station. [NOTE: do not mention that eyewitnesses' lives could be in danger if they come forward.]

SINN FÉIN

MCDONALD GROWS BEARD IN PREPARATION FOR SINN FÉIN PRESIDENCY

SMALL print contained in Sinn Féin party rules have forced incoming party president Mary Lou McDonald to begin growing a beard, WWN can reveal.

The proviso, which gives exact colour, fluffiness and length guides for the beard, is believed to have been added to party rules in recent years after attempts to discover a way to make Gerry Adams immortal failed.

McDonald is just two days into the process, but early signs are that the beard should help hardline Republicans cope with the leadership transition by the time her nomination is ratified on 10 February.

'I think the beard will ease them in; they're so used to voting for someone with a, to put it mildly, dodgy past, the fear was they'd never vote for the party if it had a leader who might only be pursuing actual policies without all the wink-wink IRA nonsense in the background,' revealed one insider with knowledge of the situation.

Senior Sinn Féin figures have admitted new leadership will also require Irish media outlets to be more creative when it comes to blatant anti-Sinn Féin rhetoric.

'The papers will have to settle for just tearing our pie-in-the-sky policies limb from limb without a mention of an IRA army council here or an IRA bombing there,' one Sinn Féin member confirmed.

It is unclear if McDonald will be required to keep the beard for the duration of her leadership or just until such time as hardline Republicans accept they can't stop the future from happening.

To coincide with McDonald's beard growth the official Sinn Féin shop is running a special 10 per cent off all Republican-themed grooming products.

Dublin Traffic:

– Dublin traffic can get incredibly busy at certain times during the day. Make a note of these times, and be sure to plan your journey to coincide with them.

– Remember cyclists break the lights all the time, the insufferable bastards. No wonder you're driven to drinking while tearing through town.

– Metro North is coming. Metro North will solve everything.

– 8 a.m. – 9.30 a.m. and 3 p.m. – 4.40 p.m. are school pick-up and drop-off times. Stay inside during these times. Lock your doors. Stock up on canned food, we don't know how long this will last.

– Should cyclists be treated with the same severity as Nazis were by the Allies in World War II? There seems to be no compelling evidence why they shouldn't be.

– Could the introduction of a fourth light on traffic lights help ease congestion? We're not sure but purple seems like a nice colour.

– Lathering Dublin's roads in Vicks VapoRub could ease congestion.

– Rush-hour Luas carriages have now replaced waterboarding as the CIA's favoured form of torture, but are operators doing enough to pack as many people on them as possible? We propose temporarily gluing commuters on the side of the carriages.

– Replace Nitelinks with Shitelinks, a cheaper form of late-night bus service that has no rules and no expectations of a decent service, therefore cutting complaints to zero.

NORTHERN IRELAND

WITH a smooth and error-free reshuffling of her cabinet completed, and news of the resignation of James Brokenshire on the grounds of ill health, Theresa May reluctantly faced up to the fact direct rule would have to return to Northern Ireland sooner rather than later, if no compromise could be reached.

However, in a move that came as a surprise to many, PM May insisted direct rule take place from Dublin and not Westminster, while trying to avoid confirming the news in a way that would confirm that she sees Northern Ireland as a massive nuisance.

'Well, we don't want to do it either, but it's your

THERESA MAY CONSIDERING DIRECT RULE FOR NORTHERN IRELAND FROM DUBLIN

responsibility now, no take backs,' May said before hastily hanging up a rushed phone call to Taoiseach Leo Varadkar.

The move to reinstate direct rule while immediately handing over the responsibility of Northern Ireland to someone else has led some to suggest the British government could potentially have little or no interest in the affairs of their citizens in the North, a claim May has strongly denied.

'Don't be upset, we'll still visit you on weekends or something. We'll work something out between ourselves and the Irish government; we promise this doesn't mean we don't love you,' May said, paraphrasing a book on how to talk to children about divorce.

'You will still be British, loved by Britain, supported by Britain, cherished by Britain, but we just won't have any direct contact with you lot, and if your name comes up on caller ID we're

going to let it ring out,' May added.

Elsewhere, Sinn Féin and the DUP have heralded recent progress in Stormont discussions after reaching an agreement on the list of things they will disagree about this week.

FUCKING WAGON

A CROSS-community poll conducted in Northern Ireland in the wake of the collapsed Stormont talks has returned a 100 per cent vote of 'fucking wagon' placed beneath a picture of DUP leader Arlene Foster, despite a polling company not providing such a possible answer, WWN can reveal.

With stumbling blocks in tense talks including an

Irish Language Act which would require hardline DUP supporters to communicate only in Irish for the next 12,000 years and the fact the DUP violently hate gay people and the very concept of actually doing their job and serving the public, many voters have expressed their frustration at a party that insists on ensuring Northern Ireland never moves forward.

'It's really easy to hate her. Sorry, that's it, there isn't a "but" part coming afterwards. It's just really easy to hate her,' confirmed one poll participant, who, at age 22, has selfishly confessed to caring more about the future of Northern Ireland than its past.

With 100 per cent of poll participants revealing 'fucking wagon' as their

official response to the breakdown of talks, some people who have clearly lost their minds have suggested that the DUP, a party which campaigned for Brexit, is against equal rights, prefers to be ruled by Westminster than reach a consensus and govern to the benefit of all of Northern Ireland, might not have everyone's best interests at heart.

No one has suggested that such a poll will do anything to help the current situation but rumours that DUP leaders have permanently erased the words 'cooperation' and 'compromise' and their synonyms from their minds isn't thought to be a positive step forward.

'It's certainly the most interesting poll I've worked

on,' confirmed veteran pollster Alan Smith. 'Despite not giving the option, those we polled also ticked, "Can you fucking please agree on something so we can actually put policies in place that will help?"'

Despite the poll's results, the DUP steadfastly maintain they will protect Unionist culture in a geographical location where it is suffocated, in the form of all public buildings carrying Union Jacks, having a currency bearing the Queen, roads, buildings and statues dedicated to its traditions and a day of marching dedicated to a Dutch-born King, William of Orange.

While the poll seems to unfairly level the blame at the feet of the leader of the DUP, no one has come forward to add anything other than 'fucking wagon'.

HOUSING

'BUILD HOMES': GENIUS MINISTER SOLVES HOUSING CRISIS

THE housing crisis is over!

A momentous day in Irish life, born out of one man's genius, as Minister for Housing Eoghan Murphy suggested Ireland look to building affordable high-rise apartments as a solution to a lack of housing units.

'Ugh, we just feel so stupid for not thinking of something like that ourselves,' chimed the nation, absolutely kicking itself for not having the same singular vision and ever-expanding wisdom of one government minister.

'So, hang on, just so we're getting this, 'cus we're a bit thick. There's not enough homes being built, and what he's saying is, we should build more? And when we're doing that we should think about building apartments and make them affordable to build and subsequently buy? Fuck, hang on, we'll need to see this written down to get it. It's a lot to take in,' added the public, marvelling at what had just been achieved by Minister Murphy and the government, who don't get enough credit sometimes.

Previously the debate and discussion around housing in Ireland was limited to

expert groups and members of the public suggesting everyone sleep on the nation's couch in the spare room. Such well-meaning solutions, however, were hampered by the fact the one couch was marginally too small to fit all the thousands of people on housing waiting lists, the homeless, and first-time buyers.

The nation, still reeling from what Minister Murphy had achieved in solving the housing crisis, made the humble suggestion that all high-rise apartments should be too small, poorly built and though named 'affordable' should be massively overpriced.

AN investigation has been launched into how the taoiseach of Ireland, Leopold Varadkar, came to be exposed to criticism while attending the People of the Year Awards, which left him fighting for his smug sense of self-satisfaction in hospital.

Rushed to hospital after being on the receiving end of criticism from People of the Year award recipient Vera Twomey, who tirelessly petitioned the government to grant a

TAOISEACH TREATED FOR SEVERE CRITICISM IN DUBLIN HOSPITAL

medicinal cannabis licence for her daughter, Taoiseach Varadkar is believed to be in a stable but severely roasted condition.

Normally protected from such direct assertions that he may not be God's gift to Irish democracy, Varadkar became visibly uncomfortable as Twomey, mother to a child whose debilitating seizures can be brought to an end with medicinal cannabis, called for the taoiseach to change the legislation regarding its use and the issuing of licences in a bid to ease the suffering of thousands of Irish citizens.

'We fucked up. We should have just kept him at home taking selfies, pretending he's watching whatever cool show people are binging on Netflix,' explained all 1,459 members of the taoiseach's extensive PR team.

The pristine social media sheen of the taoiseach's image was left severely damaged by the exchange with a normal member of the public, but it is hoped he will recover in time to never again make the mistake of attending another public event that isn't stage-managed to within an inch of its life.

'The docs gave him 10 ccs of pandering compliments and he started perking up again. But they had to lie to him and tell him a tweet of his got 1,000 retweets just to get him back on his feet, ya know,' explained a source close to the bruised ego of the taoiseach.

HEALTH

NURSES WHINGING AGAIN

A SPOKEPERSON for the government and the HSE has expressed their dismay at the fact a social media post from a psychiatric nurse, who has criticised how she and her colleagues are treated in Ireland, has gone viral, with the spokesperson careful to dismiss the post which has over 44,000 likes as just nurses whinging again.

'Well, if they have time to write and post social media whinging, they obviously aren't overworked,' confirmed the spokesperson, who is beginning to hate their job and what they stand for.

The Facebook post in question whinges endlessly about how psychiatric nurses have had to take industrial action to highlight a lack of funding, poor working conditions and understaffing.

'If we had a euro for every time a nurse moaned about how the health service is in disarray, well, we'd have enough money to fix the health service but obviously we'd spend it elsewhere anyway if we had it,' the spokesperson added.

Moaning, nagging nurses have become an annoying fixture in Irish

> ## 'Well, if they have time to write and post social media whinging, they obviously aren't overworked'

life over the last decade as they seek to irritate everyone with tales of how those in their care are rarely afforded the dignity, resources and staff levels needed to treat them, which has led to several successive governments having to waste their time and energy drawing up convincing-sounding empty promises.

This latest rant from millionaire nurses working a four-hour week comes on the third anniversary of the publication of an expert review into the Mental Health Act 2001 which made a total 165 recommendations that could transform psychiatric care in Ireland if implemented.

However, to date only one of those recommendations has

been implemented, something the government confirmed it will somehow spin into a way to praise themselves.

'One is a bigger number than zero, which, when you think about it, is a good thing,' the government spokesperson said while popping some champagne.

If you would like to know when the other 164 recommendations made by experts three years ago will be implemented you can moan and whinge like a pain-in-the-arse ungrateful nurse to the minister for mental health at jim.daly@oir.ie

Any of the 44,000 people who liked the social media post have been told if they want to organise a march on Leinster House in support of nurses, that wouldn't hurt either.

Health and Well-being Tip

Significantly reduce your alcohol intake. If this tip puts you off getting healthy, maybe just try and limit getting shitfaced to once a week. Fair play.

Vladimir Putin:

- If he's not meddling in foreign elections, he's meddling in his own election. If he's not sanctioning the poisoning and murder of people abroad, he's outright invading countries. What to do with a problem like Vlad?
- Challenge him to a bare-knuckle boxing match, proposing that, were he to lose, he would have to stop being such a bollocks. At the last minute, moments after he has oiled his body up in preparation for the fight, we replace ourselves in the fight with action movie star The Rock.
- Pushing our way to the front of a crowd of journalists asking the Russian leader questions, we propose to quietly mumble 'Dictators say what,' prompting Vladimir to fall into our meticulously laid trap. In the event he says 'What?', we may well have turned the world and humanity towards a more peaceful future. You're welcome.
- Dressing up and posing as a former Soviet Union country, we lie in wait for Putin's arrival. We then once again employ 'The Rock protocol' from a previous point once it is discovered we are not Belarus.
- Refuse all offers of being urinated on by Moscow-based prostitutes or face allowing Putin to have some leverage over you in the years to come.
- Ring Putin's office pretending to be Mother Russia. Give out to him for all the bad stuff he has done, complain about how he never visits anymore and then tell him to give up his crazy ways.
- No matter how much he insists you drink the tea he has just brewed, do not do it.

RUSSIA

'IF IT WAS US, HE'D BE DEAD'

RUSSIAN President Vladimir Putin has broken his silence today following a nerve-agent attack on the former Russian spy and double agent Sergei Skripal and his daughter Yulia, pointing to the fact that Russia would not have messed up the assassination attempt.

'I find it insulting that the international community would even suggest that we would have failed to kill Mr Skripal,' a disgruntled Mr Putin told the assembled media in Moscow today. 'We don't miss, and everyone knows this.

'If anything, this is an attack on our reputation.'

Citing previous successful assassinations, Mr Putin called on Britain's Secret Intelligence Service to send him a sample of the agent used in the attack so he can prove the chemicals used could not come from the Kremlin.

'I'm more of a polonium-210 kind of guy,' Putin added, now referring to the successful assassination of former Russian spy Alexander Litvinenko in London in 2006. 'This agent used against Skripal is inferior to anything we would use, and he would be so dead right now if it was one of our guys.

'Seriously, we're fairly good at this, and it's really bothering me that you people would believe this spy malpractice.'

Mr Putin's comments come just one day after the US expelled 60 Russian diplomats over the nerve-agent poisoning in Britain, with over a dozen EU countries following suit.

'Maybe I show you people how it's really done, to prove my point,' Putin concluded, before greenlighting today's RT headlines.

BREAKING NEWS

MAN WITH MEGAPHONE AT PROTEST THINKS HE'S NELSON MANDELA

A LOCAL man currently in possession of a megaphone at a local Waterford protest is operating under the mistaken belief that he is the second coming of Nelson Mandela.

Delivering life-changing affirmations 40 decibels louder than is needed considering the paltry crowd attendance, Declan Tanner, 35, has been preaching to his followers since the commencement of the protest earlier this morning.

Feeling the unmistakable adrenaline rush that only comes when changing society for the better, Tanner was unrelenting in his cries for society to be transformed out of its oppressive structures.

'Oh, he's been fairly excited like this now, since about 9 a.m., boi,

has the 12 or 13 people here hanging on his every very loud word,' remarked one garda deployed to the People's Park to keep an eye on Ireland's answer to one of the greatest statesmen of the 20th century.

Tanner has resisted the urge to speak without the aid of the megaphone, preferring instead to wreck the head of innocent passers with wisdom and calls for a unified and progressive society.

It is still too early to know if the impassioned campaign against an

oppressive local bin collection service and their decision to change the bin

collecting day from Monday to Tuesday will prove successful.

GOVERNMENT AWAITING US MULTINATIONALS' PERMISSION BEFORE CLOSING TAX LOOPHOLES

US multinationals based in Ireland, and of vast importance to the country's economy, have yet to give the government the final permission to close off all and any tax loopholes which greatly benefit them, WWN understands.

'We'll get back to you,' confirmed US multinationals in a joint statement, delivered via a letterbox in the foyer of a solicitor's firm operating in the IFSC area of Dublin city.

'This is a disgrace,' responded one local TD, before adding, 'we have no idea what sort of law

we have to draw up that is agreeable with these companies. It's been over a year since we asked them

to write the draft legislation for us, and still they keep the Irish people waiting. It's not on.'

US multinationals have been afforded special status in Ireland in recent years after middle-class people with decent jobs explained that you're not allowed to ask companies to pay

the correct levels of tax, confirming that any such requests are 'downright rude'.

'That's all well and good, loonies on the left saying they should pay appropriate taxes but then what? Are they just expected to stay in the country and figure out a business model which doesn't require continuously ignoring the laws of the countries they're based in? You fucking crackpots,' remarked one man, who would know a great deal more about serious things like this than you do.

Once the government gets permission to close the loopholes, the subsequent legislation then goes before the houses of the Oireachtas and is debated at committee stage before finally being placed in a bin and forgotten about.

HUNCHBACKED BEAST FROTHING AT MOUTH CLAIMS TO BE YOUR LOCAL ELECTION CANDIDATE

A MANGLED, indistinguishable assemblage of limbs which utters grunts and foams at the mouth while attempting to say 'new roads' is claiming to be a local candidate for any and all future elections in your area.

'Jobs,' the hunchback said, launching endless streams of spittle from its mouth, as it placed an election campaign leaflet in your hand.

'Vote … me,' implored the decrepit abomination.

'You vote,' the beast grunted. 'You vote me,' it added, clearly starting out on a journey to mastering the basics of human speech.

'I job for the area,' added the sight for sore eyes, not flinching even when its arm detached from its body.

The sensational entry of the hunchbacked beast frothing at the mouth has upended the political landscape in the local area, with the beast currently polling at 86 per cent favourable amongst voters in the area.

'It seems like a decent fella, wants to bring jobs to the area and you can't say fairer than that. It has my vote,' one local man remarked.

'THE INTERNET IS EXPOSING OUR LIES AND IT NEEDS TO STOP'

PHILANTHROPISTS, lobbyists, financiers, CEOs and world leaders all gathered at the World Economic Forum in Davos this week to discuss the risks posed by too much information being funnelled down to the lower classes via the internet and social media channels.

Speaking with their mouths, political leaders lined up to slam social networks for gaining more power than they do, insisting that investors should boycott social media platforms that don't delete and censor perceived views that are not in line with their own.

'Facebook has more influence and reach than any world government, and that's bad,' British Prime Minister Theresa May insisted. 'The lower classes now have the ability to see every mistake we make and every unedited lie uttered in real time.

'How are we supposed to divide and conquer if all the lower classes are joined together in harmony under one single global platform?' she then asked a now flabbergasted audience of megalomaniac billionaires and world leaders. 'Even the working class are starting to read the news, news that we didn't create or sign off on with Rupert, news that's exposing many of our secrets – fake news.'

Echoing the British leader's remarks, philanthropist George Soros, who is allegedly connected to over 50 'real news' publications, said Facebook and Google have become 'obstacles to innovation' and are a 'menace' to society whose 'days are numbered'.

'When it comes to information, we cannot entrust people lesser than us with the ability to make their own decisions,' said the 87-year-old, who spends millions of euro every year influencing people's opinions for the financial gain of himself and his peers. 'These social networks allow the lower classes to share their own information, thus influencing how people think and behave around us – which is kinda our job.'

'Facebook has given the power of the media to the people, and now they're using it against us by exposing our lies and giving them the ability to ask questions publicly; this needs to stop before they start getting any big ideas, like forcing the 1 per cent to share our wealth with those who need it,' Soros concluded, before bowing to a standing ovation from the world elite.

BREAKING NEWS

BORIS JOHNSON RUSHED TO HOSPITAL WITH SUSPECTED HEAD UP ARSE

BRITISH Foreign Secretary Boris Johnson was rushed to a London hospital in the last hour with a suspected head up arse, believed to be his own, sources have confirmed.

Mr Johnson reportedly collapsed shortly after delivering a key speech on Brexit, before curling up into a ball and succumbing to his own anus.

'He mumbled something like, "unite about what we all believe in",' eyewitness and journalist James Carran told WWN. 'He just became very incoherent after that, presumably because the lining of his anal passage absorbed most of his bullshit – it was quite the sight to behold.

'I've never seen someone's head turn into themselves like that, but it seemed to be at home up there, and fitted right in.'

'He just became very incoherent after that, presumably because the lining of his anal passage absorbed most of his bullshit'

Emergency services arrived shortly after Mr Johnson's collapse and managed to get a breathing apparatus to his mouth before he suffocated on the remnants of yesterday's lobster dinner.

'This is not the first time Boris's head has retracted up his own hole,' a government source explained.

'We usually just jimmy it out with a wooden spoon, but sometimes his head swells so big after delivering a speech, it's just impossible to wedge anything else up there.'

Doctors have voiced major concerns for Johnson's long-term health as they identified his continuous claiming that Brexit is the greatest British achievement of all time to be the leading cause of his head-up-arse condition.

Suburban Dictionary

'Sleeveen' – a sly or cunning person, or a person named 'Stephen' when pronounced by someone who has had about 9 pints.

BREXIT

WHERE ARE THEY NOW? THE BREXIT BUS

THE bus slogan that will live in infamy: 'We send the EU £350 million a week, let's fund our NHS instead – Vote Leave'.

Many commentators maintain that the evocative message emblazoned on the side of the German-manufactured Neoplan Skyliner bus swung Britain's referendum to leave the EU in the favour of the Leave side, plunging Britain into a period of uncertainty, embarrassment and economic peril.

While many point the finger of blame at Nigel Farage, Boris Johnson or other similarly annoying toffs, the question persists as to the role of the bus itself and where exactly the traitorous pro-Leave vehicle resides today.

WWN went in search of answers. It was surprisingly easy to find them.

After a quick search of the EU-controlled internet, which limits what you can search in the UK, porn-

wise, thanks to a decision solely taken by the then Cameron-led government, we discovered the bus did the daily route from Bournemouth to Swanage.

'I don't want any London-based routes, it just brings back horrible memories and I get recognised, shouted at,' purred the engine of the Neoplan Skyliner, Neo for short, when we confronted him. 'Last time I got clamped while stopped at a zebra crossing. You know it's bad when bastard clampers think you're a shit too.

'Still get recognised round here in Bournemouth, but I just switch into the bus lane and floor it,' Neo hummed, as he explained no matter how many power hoses he is washed by, you can still make out the remnants of the '£350 million' portion of the dreaded false claim.

Being recognised doesn't always involve an aggressive response – sometimes Neo is greeted with cheers.

'It's tough having fans you don't really want, being famous for something you're not proud of. It's basically like being Nigel Farage. I can beep in a kind response, give them a wave of the wipers but like Nigel, I think they're all cunts really,' added Neo, who feels like his life has been

> ## 'I don't want any London-based routes, it just brings back horrible memories and I get recognised, shouted at'

stuck in reverse ever since he agreed to carry the slogan.

Neo rejects notions that he should have fact-checked the claims himself.

'I was designed in Germany and built in Poland. English is my third language, the nuances of the language escape me sometimes,' Neo defended, while revving his engine defensively.

Remorse, regret, remain. All the Rs Neo feels have led him to some dark places which he was kind enough to share with WWN.

'In my darkest days I tried to drive to a scrap yard but the guy recognised me and wouldn't put me in the crusher. I begged him but nothing. Sometimes I brake sharply at green lights just to feel the car behind hit me, but really it just feels like nothing now,' Neo explained before breaking down on the hard shoulder, inconsolable.

GOVERNMENT AWARDS DENIS O'BRIEN WITH 'THE BENEFIT OF THE DOUBT' IN TOUCHING CEREMONY

IN lieu of any indication that An Garda Síochána will act on or investigate the findings of the Moriarty Tribunal, and in an attempt to save the public money associated with the cost of the tribunal examining the sale of SiteServ, the government has given Denis O'Brien the benefit of the doubt in a ceremony described by onlookers as 'deeply moving'.

The ceremony took place at Dublin Castle and was attended by the great and good of Ireland's business community, with many present remarking how they too looked forward to taking part in a similar ceremony when the time comes.

A lavish dinner, attended by no one in the lower tax bracket, thank God, was said to have brought a tear to many people's eyes as speech after speech, delivered in the banquet hall of the castle, spoke of a bright future in which other tribunal participants could enjoy being bestowed with one of the greatest honours Irish politicians can administer.

'We as a country rarely value the contribution made by people in Ireland, and its endlessly glorious history, but even I, an often-harsh critic of the exceptionally gifted government, can say this is a long-overdue award,' confirmed an editorial in the *Irish Independent*, which WWN understands was not written by someone held at gunpoint.

Unfortunately, Mr O'Brien was unable to attend the ceremony itself as he is resident in Malta, but it is believed a team of 87 solicitors attended in his absence.

LEGAL

NEW COURT BUILT JUST TO DEAL WITH DENIS O'BRIEN'S LEGAL CASES

CITING the demands put on courts by previous, current and future court cases in which billionaire Denis O'Brien is involved, the decision has been made to build the Denis O'Brien Claims Court in Dublin, WWN can reveal.

With the volume of past, present and future litigation taken by or against the Digicel businessman, the need for a special dedicated court to begin operating had been flagged for some time.

'Denis has nine stamps on his "Take nine cases to court, get your 10th free" loyalty card. So we'd be happy to represent him whenever some toys need throwing out of a pram,' confirmed a legal consultant with a firm that has represented O'Brien in the past.

The Denis O'Brien Claims Court will have 14 individual courtrooms, operating simultaneously, allowing the Maltese tax resident to seamlessly move from room to room and case to case, rendering all legal proceedings into an easily manageable conveyor belt-style operation.

'Ah God, the hassle we'll save with this. It'll be great,' remarked one judge who was happy he might finally get a case not involving someone making claims for or against the billionaire who was found by the Moriarty Tribunal to have made two payments to then Fine Gael Minister Michael Lowry in 1996 and 1999 totalling IR£500,000 (GB£147,000 and GB£300,000) and supported a loan of GB£420,000 given to Lowry in 1999, a benefit equivalent to a payment, when bidding for the state's second mobile phone licence.

Gardaí have been told that were these findings to be acted upon, any eventual case would have to take place in the DBCC, which is scheduled to begin construction shortly.

EXCLUSIVE

HOMELESS TO BE BROKEN UP INTO 'HOMELESS' AND 'REALLY FUCKING HOMELESS'

IN a bid to lower the bad look of the country's current homelessness crisis, the government has unveiled a scheme which will break up statistics into people living in emergency accommodation and people living rough on the streets.

There are currently some 8,200 homeless men, women and children in Ireland today, which the government claims is 'a poor representation' of the amount of people who are 'really, really fucking homeless'.

Current figures put the number of rough sleepers in the Dublin area at around 160, with no official figures for the rest of the country, which 'can't be that much higher' according to a think tank in Leinster House.

This lower figure will be the one put forward on a yearly basis as Ireland's official tally of homeless

people, with Taoiseach Leo Varadkar said to be very pleased that he has lowered the number of homeless people by 8,000 in just his first year in office.

'If we put forward just the number of people who are actually bottom-of-the-well derelict as being "homeless", then it doesn't really look all that bad,' said a spokesperson for the government, looking up and down the street to see if there were any dead homeless people on the doorstep today.

'As for the families in emergency accommodation, we just need to find a new name for them, something else, such as "families in emergency accommodation". That might do the job. They're not 'homeless homeless', like the lads you see lying in sleeping bags on doorsteps. We just split the two groups, and call it a win!'

So far, the public appears to be getting on board with the plan to stop counting people in emergency accommodation who aren't 'really fucking homeless', and have praised the government for their good work.

Parish Notes

This week's parish lotto jackpot is on course to top €11.50.

CIVIL SERVANT CAN'T REMEMBER THE LAST TIME HE DID A REAL DAY'S WORK

ASKED by a team of researchers conducting a work productivity survey, 'When was the last time you did a decent day's work?', one civil servant was left scratching his head and admitting to having no knowledge of any such alleged incident, WWN can confirm.

Trevor Dowding, placed in a quiet corner of the Department of Finance since 1991 where his superiors are fairly certain he can do no damage, was posed the question earlier this morning and has been left searching his memory ever since.

'No, you'd think alright with 2008 and what hit then and everything that followed that I'd have had to up my game, but surprisingly enough I still can't remember the last time I broke

a sweat in this place,' Dowding said with a chuckle and a content shrug of the shoulders.

While the vast majority of the civil service is engaged in hard and meaningful work despite the presence of a government, Dowding is believed to be part of the small minority of personnel who have breezed through a career of doing a whole heap of nothing.

'Wait, wait, wait, the wife had me book a holiday to France there last

'I still can't remember the last time I broke a sweat in this place'

year on the computer when I was in work, does non-work stuff count? I had to tick the carry-on luggage box and everything,' Dowding asked, genuinely curious if five minutes on Ryanair's website was the sort of thing researchers were looking for.

Dowding, helpful to a fault, then began searching through previous emails before highlighting a Monday in March of 2006 when he sent as many as six emails.

'Christ, I'd say I hit the hay pretty early that evening, not sure what sort of shit hit the fan that day,' Dowding remarked, cursing himself for not being able to recall internal emails to colleagues in which he tried to identify the person who took the last of the communal Jaffa Cakes in the canteen.

GARDA BREATHLYSER REVEALED TO BE EMPTY RIBENA CARTONS

THE garda breathalyser scandal took another turn today, after it was revealed that the equipment being used by roadside gardaí to check motorists was actually an empty cardboard juice box with some buttons drawn on the side.

The revelation goes some way to explaining why statistics for nearly two million breath tests that never took place were lodged by gardaí over the course of a decade, as the tests seldom took place using an actual breathalyser.

Members of a special committee set up to get to the bottom of the scandal once and for all made the discovery after interviewing a number of people whose names and vehicle registration details showed up on the system, and subsequently suggested that poor garda funding meant that almost 100 per cent of tests were carried out using a Ribena carton.

'I remember thinking, this tastes a bit blackcurrant-y,' said one motorist, who preferred to remain anonymous.

'The guard said, "Keep blowing until I say stop." I could just see the carton expanding; I'm thinking this thing is going to fucking pop. You couldn't see it was a Ribena box because they'd drawn all over it in marker. Then the guard just said "Okay, you can go on now," and pretended to be pushing buttons on the carton.'

The findings come just days after it was revealed that the garda supply of pepper spray is actually just silly string.

'EVEN GREENER PARTY' LAUNCHES TO RIVAL GREEN PARTY

THE Eamon Ryan-led Green Party are facing complete destruction after the launch of a rival, more environmentally motivated political party, the 'Even Greener Party'.

Operating with a policy of waiting for the Green Party to release new policies and stances before going even further, the Even Greener Party has attracted climate change activists to its base by claiming to hug more trees than the once-upon-a-time minority party in government.

'They say they want to save animals from cruelty such as being hunted for sport, but they never give a number. The Even Greener Party probably wants to save even more animals,' Even Greener Party leader Barry Prevette confirmed to the wild applause of a crowd of supporters.

Prevette also outlined how good he is at putting the green bin out, before launching a new bike-centred policy which could draw further attention away from the Green Party to his nascent movement.

'Every baby will get a free bike and wind turbine on their first birthday. Now, I'd like to see the Green Party match that,' explained Prevette.

Such impressive pronouncements have seen the Even Greener Party corner the market when it comes to attracting members who carve wind chimes in their spare time while talking about how much damage cows' bowel movements do to the environment.

WW news

Waterford Whispers News

LOCAL NEWS

TECHNOLOGY

COULD A RED COW CATAPULT BE THE ANSWER TO DUBLIN'S COMMUTER PROBLEM?

WITH yet even more delays on Ireland's most congested motorway, the M50, WWN takes a look at some of the more alternative ways a commuter can gain access to the city centre in time for work.

At the Red Cow interchange on the outskirts of the city we meet up with entrepreneur Thomas Holden, whose Red Cow Catapult has been in full operation since 2016 and caters for 1,300 commuters every day.

'It might not seem a lot, but it's early days yet,' Thomas explains while securing a middle-aged businessman into one of four giant catapults that are strategically pointed at the city centre. 'We had a few hiccups at the start due to crosswinds and that, but we've finally mastered it,' he says, before pulling a lever and sending the man several hundred feet

---

'We had a few hiccups at the start due to crosswinds and that, but we've finally mastered it'

---

into the air before disappearing out of sight.

'As the crow flies, he should land in the Liffey outside Heuston station in about 2 minutes,' Holden confirms, loading another commuter. 'We have spotters on the other side, ready to take them out of the river; it's the quickest way into town.'

Travelling at 150 miles an hour over the packed city streets seems insane, almost ludicrous, but like any frustrated commuter, this reporter was willing to give it a go.

'Just put yourself into a foetal position and you'll be fine,' the entrepreneur advises as he hands me my briefcase and a signed contract that waives my rights as a human being. 'And whatever you do, hold on tight to

your belongings as an iMac Pro took out a cyclist last May. We don't take any responsibility for that kind of thing so if you can sign your name here we'll send you on your way.'

Literally seconds after dotting the 'i' in my name, I'm catapulted into the air over the adjacent JFK industrial estate. The velocity creates a wind which makes it hard to breathe and I begin hyperventilating. I can feel myself starting to spin around the halfway mark, over Drimnagh, as I begin my descent towards Heuston Station. The time seems to drag as images from my life flash before me, before I splash down, narrowly missing the bridge that brings you onto Wolf Tone Street, where a team of 'catchers' wait.

One thing I wasn't expecting was the pain from hitting the water so hard. I dislocated my shoulder, but remembering the static traffic below on my journey made it worth it. Also, I was drowned wet, but all in all, it's a good way into the city and I would highly recommend it to anyone willing to fork over the €400 fare.

Bottom line: the Red Cow Catapult does exactly what it says on the tin. 8/10.

WORK COLLEAGUE CAN GIVE IT, BUT CAN'T TAKE IT

FOR Cathal Murphy, having the bants with friends and work colleagues is what life is all about; that is, however, until someone bants him back, a source close to the man has confirmed to WWN.

'He usually picks on people that he knows won't fight back,' exasperated work colleague Theresa Hayes explains. 'He's not even funny and basically just repeats the same tired old jests and one-liners all the time. Everyone in the office is just sick of him.

'The thing is, when someone does retaliate with even the mildest of retorts, he throws a strop that can sometimes last for hours, even days,' she added.

In one instance last week, the 'office joker' pranked fellow work colleague James Howard by covering his office cubicle in yellow Post-it notes while he was in a work training module.

'Fair enough, James shat in Cathal's bin when he went out for a smoke, but his reaction when he came back was uncalled for,' said fellow team member Hazel McCormack, referring to how Cathal later emptied the bin's runny contents over an office fan, which was at full power, facing Mr Howard at the time.

'Bottom line here is when the shit hits the fan, James can give it, but he can't take it,' she concluded.

BREAKING

DRUG GANGS OFFICIALLY THANK IRISH PUBLIC FOR CONTINUED SUPPORT

A CONGLOMERATE of national drug gangs officially thanked the Irish public for their continued support over the past 30 years at their annual AGM in a Dublin city hotel this afternoon.

Boasting billion-euro profits year-on-year, cartel bosses and henchmen donning balaclavas and flanked by armed personnel also thanked the sitting press and the Irish government for their part in their ongoing reign of violence and terror, stating that they couldn't have done it without them.

'We would really like to thank the *Sunday World* for their continued glamourising of our key players by giving them nicknames and reporting their wealth. Recruiting disadvantaged young men has never been easier,' said one boss, before turning to attending Justice Minister Charles Flanagan and winking at him. 'And, of course, we couldn't have done any of this without the government's incompetence and continued cuts on the Garda Síochána, whose corruption, may I add, is quite an inspiration to

Parish Notes

Congratulations to Fr Hartin, who recently won a free trip to another parish, where he has decided to stay forever and no more questions should be asked about the matter.

everyone working in our criminal network.'

'If not for your right-wing stance on cannabis, we wouldn't be making a third of the money we are now. So well done on keeping that plant illegal, despite its vast array of medical benefits – making criminals out of normal people is usually our job, but I won't complain,' he added, before pulling out a semi-automatic pistol and firing it three times in the air.

'And finally, three cheers for the Irish public; without your love of cocaine and your indifference to the fact you fund our bloodshed, we wouldn't be here today… Hip, hip, hooray!' he shouted, between gunfire. 'Hip, hip, hooray!'

METAL DETECTORIST DISCOVERS HOARD OF ROMAN BITCOINS WORTH €10 MILLION IN FARMER'S FIELD

A LONG-lost hoard of Roman bitcoins believed to be worth millions of euro has been found in a farmer's field in Devon, UK, WWN can confirm.

The collection of nearly 1,600 bitcoin was found buried in the ground by metal detectorist Philip Hayward while he was scanning a local field in his area which is known by historians to be the location of a Roman cryptocurrency mine, dating back to the year AD 334.

The cryptocoins, featuring Roman Emperor Constantine the Great and members of his family, are said to be worth almost €10 million in today's money, with the purse to be split evenly between the owner of the field and Mr Hayward.

'To say I'm ecstatic is an understatement,' Hayward told WWN. 'I've been searching these fields for over 12 years now in the hope of finding exactly where the bitcoin mine was located, and I believe there are probably dozens of similar mine locations around the UK that still have yet to be discovered.'

Each bitcoin currently trades for €6,075 at the time of writing, but due to its increasing value, it could be worth a lot more in years to come.

'When you think about the fact that one bitcoin was worth as little as €1 eight years ago, it makes you want to hold off a bit before selling them on,' added Hayward. 'I might just hold on to them for another few years to see if the currency keeps rising in value.'

Bitcoin was first discovered by the Egyptian Pharaoh Ramesses III over three thousand years ago, who later used enormous complex structures called pyramids to house and mine the cryptocurrency.

SELF-SERVICE TILL SUPERVISOR HAVING CHAT AT OTHER END OF STORE

AT any one time, the majority of self-service till supervisors are having a little chat with their work colleagues at the other end of the store, a new real-time survey into self-service till supervisors has revealed.

Right now, approximately 97 per cent of supervisors are being hailed by the self-service checkout machines as thousands of customers desperately pan across the busy shop floor in a bid to lock eyes with the person who is meant to be in charge.

The report found that the majority of the missing supervisors are probably talking to one of the real checkout girls about the new manager, Brian, while casually laughing and joking in a complacent manner, almost taunting customers now waiting in a large queue.

Despite the fact that not one customer in the history of self-service checkouts has successfully managed to scan their shopping without having to hail a supervisor, it seems the majority of operators still continue to disappear from their work station duties on a regular basis.

'Maybe if self-service till attendants stayed where they were supposed to, there would be fewer queues,' the groundbreaking report concluded.

Following the survey, it is expected that new measures will be introduced to the self-service checkout tills, including new automated messages, such as:

'Help is on its way, in about 10 minutes after Noreen tells Jessica all about John-from-the-deli-department's breakup with the missus.'

'There's an unexpected little shit leaning on the baggage area.'

'Don't forget to scan that bag, we're watching you.'

'This is card only, you gobshite.'

'Don't forget your phone credit again for the 100th time.'

A NEW television licensing system unveiled at RTÉ studios today by Minister for Communications Denis Naughton will now force viewers wishing to avail of the broadcasting service to undergo a theory test for a provisional, and a practical test for a full television licence.

Learner viewers will have to sit for a 45-minute test on basic television rules and regulations of the TV industry, including complex BAI guidelines, before they can go on to apply for a full television licence, which will entail passing a practical test at a designated TV licence test centre.

'Successful learner permit holders will only be allowed access to two basic TV stations, RTÉ 1 and RTÉ 2 for €255 per year,' Mr Naughton explained. 'Full television licence holders will gain access to all the Irish TV stations for as little €155 per year, which is an amazing €10 cheaper than it is now.'

Wonderful World of Science

A number of scientists cowering in a heap while clutching their faces can confirm getting poked in the eye hurts.

GOVERNMENT TO INTRODUCE PROVISIONAL TV LICENCE FOR LEARNER VIEWERS

The new licensing system follows renewed calls from the state broadcaster to increase the licence fee in a bid to cover the huge deficits at the station, with director general Dee Forbes welcoming the boost in revenue.

'This couldn't have come at a better time,' Forbes pointed out. 'We were very close to sacking the commissioning editors, producers and union-protected staff responsible for RTÉ's decline over the past couple of decades. Now we can keep them all in their roles and continue ignoring the fact that television is a dying medium destined to collapse due to our failures to properly migrate the service into the 21st century,' adding, 'we might even update the

RTÉ Player to the year 2008, and see if we can get some internet "hits" all these hip young folk keep talking about these days.'

The new licence system is expected to cost the taxpayer in the region of €12 billion euro over the next four years and generate an extra €500,000 a year for RTÉ.

'We're also looking into compulsory TV testing, where owners will have to bring in their TV sets to be tested for wave worthiness,' Naughton explained. 'This, of course, is more of a safety concern than a revenue concern.'

All provisional TV licence holders will be required to show an L-plate on their front window for inspectors to see.

BREAKING

'YOU'RE WELCOME,' MIDDLE CLASS TELL CHRISTMAS BONUS RECIPIENTS

'We don't want the poor upper classes feeling in any way obliged to contribute to society. They have enough on their plate'

IN a rare nod to the unemployed population of Ireland, the nation's middle class took out front page adverts on all the national newspapers today to simply say 'You're welcome' to recipients of this year's dole Christmas bonus, despite never actually receiving any thanks in the first place, WWN can confirm.

A sum of €220 million in Christmas bonus social welfare payments will be paid out this week to some 1.2 million people, made up of pensioners, people with disabilities, carers, lone parents, long-term unemployed people and various other recipients.

'It's just a friendly reminder to let them know that we're not in any way bitter about our hard-earned taxes being used to pay for their bonuses and weekly welfare payments,'

explained small-business owner Gerry Hope, who is also head of the Middle Class Association of Ireland. 'No, really, we all get it up here. It's fine if some entrepreneurs work 70 hours a week, creating jobs and struggling to meet their large tax bill every quarter. No animosity there at all. In my eyes, there's no class divide.'

The small print belonging to the full page advert, under the headline, 'YOU'RE WELCOME', in bold capital letters, went on to address the upper classes and multinationals in Ireland, telling them, 'No, you're fine. We've got this,' referring to the low tax bills many on the upper tier in modern-day Irish society pay.

'Look, we don't want the poor upper classes feeling in any way obliged to contribute to society.

Did You Know?

Bare-knuckle boxing bouts often involved bears until Microsoft Word's spellcheck feature was invented.

They have enough on their plate and have obviously worked hard to get where they are,' added Hope. 'The middle class will gladly take care of all the silly things like the health department, social housing, infrastructure. Let them keep churning in that cash. I'm sure it will be put to good use, some day.'

The bonus – paid at the rate of 85 per cent of a person's normal weekly payment – will be made to over 630,000 pensioners and 580,000 other social welfare recipients.

EXCLUSIVE

LOCAL MAN NEVER GOES OUT NEW YEAR'S

A COUNTY Waterford man has left family members, friends and neighbours speechless today following an announcement which has left many questioning his life choices after claiming to never go out on New Year's Eve.

Despite it being collectively celebrated by billions of people around the world, David Kennedy slammed New Year's Eve as a 'sham', stating he would rather spend it at home alone watching Jools Holland on TV.

'It's only another day to me,' Kennedy scoffed, blissfully unaware of the impact of his words. 'Load of bollocks is all it is; bunch of children getting sick everywhere, shiftin' the faces off themselves, queuing for pints all night, everyone fucked out then on the street at half two killing each other… sure, where's the enjoyment in that?

'New Year's me hole!' he added.

David's full-time sister, Sarah Kennedy, revealed she had no idea her brother had gotten to that stage in his life already, admitting to not knowing what to do about his choice not to go out tonight.

'He's 38 years old, so I suppose we should have seen this coming,' she explained, now holding an old photograph of David in happier times of his life. 'What next? He'll stop going to weddings, funerals, Christmas dinners? Like, where does it end?'

Asked whether he ever enjoyed a New Year's night out, Kennedy replied: 'The last New Year's I went out was 2000. Now, there was a proper countdown to the unknown; sure, we all thought we were gonna die when the clock struck 12, so we made sure to give it a good aul fucking lash, neckin' yokes and snortin' K. It's all this flowery PC bollocks now with fuckers holding hands and pretending to be happy.'

In a recent report, eight out of ten thirty-somethings in Ireland admitted to not going out New Year's Eve due to the town being 'too packed' and being unable to hear their friends talk about themselves.

Summer on the 39

Memoirs of an undercover Spanish student

Chapter Two:

I have been in Ireland now for the last week, and the family in Blanchardstown who I am staying with think I am just a regular Spanish student, here to learn English. They do not know that I am really here to learn the inner workings of the 39A bus route, so that my people back home can implement these learnings to our own infrastructure. To maintain the illusion that I am just a teenage boy and not a 37-year-old Spanish file clerk, I must study my fellow exchange students and do exactly as they do. It took a while to get the hang of it, but I have mastered the art of walking down a pavement four abreast, stopping abruptly every so often in complete unison with my friends, so that we create an impassable wall of Spanish adolescence that impedes every other pedestrian at random intervals. I had been worried that my English would not be strong enough to make me believable as a student on an exchange specifically designed to help me learn English, but it turns out to be no problem – none of the students ever make any attempt to speak anything other than Spanish, at the highest volume they can muster. That reminds me, I must do my vocal warm-ups before I leave for today's excursion. The constant screaming is killing my throat. I am drinking honey and lemon almost as fast as my fellow students are drinking Coca-Cola mixed with red wine.

Suburban Dictionary

'The Leaving Cert' – often confused for the Leaving Certificate, the Leaving Cert is actually short for leaving, certainly, and heading to Australia as fast as possible.

CHOOSING THE MOST OFFENSIVE IMAGE FOR YOUR PRO-LIFE CAMPAIGN POSTER

FORCING your opinions on people can sometimes be hard, unforgiving work, as not everyone seems to be as well educated and informed on the inner workings of modern day society as you, so choosing the right disturbing image to sway their underdeveloped minds is key to winning this farce of a referendum.

Compiled below are some key campaign poster guidelines every pro-life supporter should read before setting out on the campaign trail.

1) The aborted foetus

This tried and tested imagery is an old favourite of many a pro-life group and it really packs a punch. Best kept for big marches, these posters must be large and of a high resolution, no lower than 300 dpi, to send home the message that people who carry out and opt for this medical procedure are nasty, evil butchers with no regard for human life. Shove the images in people's faces when they least expect it by placing them in busy city streets, making sure to have no regard for the personal history or viewpoints of the passersby. Remember, this is all about you, and how you personally feel about the subject of abortion. Make sure to stick your fingers in your ears when individual cases where the pregnant woman's life was at risk are put to you. Fob off such stories as 'pro-choice propaganda', while shoving the chopped up foetus picture in their killer faces. Septicaemia what?

Why don't you just let God handle your poisoned blood and let him decide if you should live or die, murderer! You don't see the rest of us relying on modern science.

2) Someone posing as a nurse

Sometimes you've got to bend the rules a little when it comes to serious situations like a national abortion referendum. And we're pretty sure God would overlook something as trivial as using a fake abortion nurse with a pre-planned script to manipulate people with scaremongering tales from the abortion floor, considering all the other things carried out in his name that he has somehow overlooked in the last two thousand odd years. There's no harm in a little white lie here or there. For example, aren't those dentists on the toothpaste adverts all actors? Same too with those insurance claim advert people. We're not technically 'lying' lying; it's a campaign for Christ's sakes, a multimillion-euro campaign funded largely by foreign, right-wing Christian fundamentalist groups and lobbyists like George Soros. Nothing cloak and dagger here, thank you very much. So yeah, manipulation of the truth is okay as long as it benefits your pro-life agenda. We've got your back.

3) Something that has zero relevance

Have a good look around for some condition you can use to scare people with and dishonestly link to a referendum about removing or keeping the Eighth Amendment in the Constitution. Disabilities are great for tugging on and manipulating the heart strings, especially disabilities that people are born with, like Down's syndrome. Sure, our Church used to stick people with disabilities into special homes and some were sexually, physically and mentally abused before being dumped into septic tanks, but thankfully Down's syndrome kids have finally found their purpose in life: your pro-life campaign poster. Don't lose focus and try to campaign for increased supports, funding and outlets for people with disabilities, just stick with slapping them on a poster. Obviously, caring for humans after they're born isn't our bag, but caring for our point of view being shoved down people's throats is.

4) More aborted foetuses

When all else fails, stick to the classics.

'WHAT IF JESUS HAD BEEN ABORTED?'

In his latest column, Bishop Cornelius Byle, WWN's resident priest and conscience expert, poses the question which is absolutely central and crucial to the reasoned debate on the factual matter of murderous mass genocide of children.

GOOD after-morning to you all and welcome to my column. I must start off with an apology as in my last column, I may have suggested children born with certain afflictions had been punished by God for the sins of their parents but I realise now that, although I believe it deep within my heart, it's not really helpful to me or certain current debates to broadcast that opinion.

Now that my most sincere apology is out of the way I'll just cut to the chase: what if Jesus had been aborted by you mentally deranged feminists? What then, huh? What. Then.

Aha, just as I thought. Cat got your disgusting tongue. Game, set and match, Bishop Byle.

Jesus, famously, was Jesus Christ himself, and what's more he was once a baby. Additional moreness, he was also in Mary's womb, ergo, you genocidal maniacs would have killed him.

I don't need to labour this point obviously, but all experts accept that science and medicine have no place in the debate surrounding the health of babies when they are living inside the ticking time bomb of what we refer to notionally as 'a woman'.

Now, the soulless hell-bound cataclysms you tend to refer to as 'my mother', 'my sister', 'my daughter', 'my partner' or 'my friend' are asking you to vote in a referendum about whether or not we should vote to abort baby Jesus Christ. They can deny it, but it's a

fact. Just look at the factual ads in your newsfeeds and on posters which are not fearmongering. That's such a twisting of what I'm doing. I'm doing something far more joyful: I am in fact terror-informing.

Cast your ears and eyes away from unhelpful terms like 'facts' and 'truth' and instead just concentrate on this: 'What if Jesus had been born aborted?' Since I'm not entirely sure where I'm going with this line of thinking, please consider this thought for a moment if you would be so kind: 'No, seriously, what if Jesus had been aborted?'

I've been asked by sinful people why I'm so vocal about an issue like this, but so silent on Fr Burrition who was moved from my

parish after 20 years of… you know? Or about how the church ran Mother and Baby homes and allegedly sold children illegally and enslaved vulnerable women in workhouses? Or how there's the odd harmless mass grave here and there. Or about how children outside the womb are treated? It's all just very convenient nit picking.

And technically, people can ask those questions, since the gardaí, possibly in league with the Devil, don't consider that a crime apparently, and just let them ask those awkward questions, willy-nilly.

Now, please burn the contents of this article immediately after reading it. Your bodily desires disgust me.

WORRYING REPORTS OF YOUNG PEOPLE TURNING OUT TO VOTE

WITH polling stations only open a few hours, a number of news outlets are already reporting the truly horrific sight of hordes of young people casting their votes, WWN can confirm.

'Oh God no, they're exercising their democratic right in order to shape Ireland into a better place for women,' screamed one No campaigner as he paced back and forth.

The sight of young men and women casting their

votes and subsequently talking online about how good it felt to possibly play a part in pushing Ireland towards becoming a more caring place for women with crisis pregnancies after 35 years under the Eighth Amendment has forced many No campaigners to question if democracy is needed at all.

'And some of them don't even look Irish,' added a middle-aged No voter while staring at legitimate Irish

citizens, as he suddenly warmed to the idea of restricting the right to vote to just a select few people he could pre-approve after a lengthy screening process.

Previous elections and referendums have occasionally seen a similar trend of young people mistakenly thinking their own opinions and views carry as much importance as those of older people who have more life experience. Sadly, there are

no current plans to raise the voting age to 45 where it clearly needs to be.

Worse still is the news that young people are fully conscious of just how important having and using their vote can be.

'That's history in your hands,' remarked one visibly emotional young person to a friend, clearly one of those artsy types who tends to over sentimentalise dismantling onerous and dysfunctional legislation which has caused minor, harmless, barely noticeable suffering to generations of Irish women.

NOT VOTING ON FRIDAY? HERE'S HOW TO MAKE YOUR OPINION KNOWN ANYWAY

WITH only days to go before Ireland heads to the polls to decide the fate of the eighth, many Irish people are leaving the decision in the hands of people who are actually planning on voting, but that doesn't mean that they can't have their say on the matter in the meantime.

'It's a real pain in my hole to go all the way back to Westmeath to vote,' said Dublin-based man George Wilten, who meant to get his polling address changed but never bothered.

'But yeah, I'd recommend everyone to vote to repeal the eighth, not that I have to, it's kind of a done deal at this stage. Did you see the latest polling figures? The Yes side is way ahead. So even if I could vote on Friday, there'd be no need anyways.'

Like a huge portion of the electorate, Wilten has opted to remove himself from the voting process in order to be able to enjoy his Friday without any needless stress, travel or inconvenience, but remains confident that the eighth will pass due to poll numbers that rival those of Hillary Clinton or the 'remain' movement in the days before voting.

If you yourself feel like a day off on Friday, but still want to make your opinions on the matter known, then there are options open to you:

1) Social media
You don't have to actually vote to make a difference in this referendum; you can just post your views on Twitter or Facebook. There's bound to be enough people voting to actually win the damn thing, so all you have to do is sit back and get some sweet retweets from the side of your choosing. Remember, the side that gets the most clout on Twitter is the side that will win! That's how democracy works!

2) Tell everyone how you would vote, if you were going to
If you can't make it to the polls on Friday because meh, effort, then you can do just as much good for the movement of your choice by bringing the referendum into conversation as often as you can, stating your preference, and then moving on. You don't have to tell people that you're not going to actually, you know, vote. They're not going to follow you into the voting booth, are they? It's called lying, and it can get you out of pretty much anything in life, including crucial referendums that will shape the future of this country.

3) Criticise early, criticise often
Even though you've got plans on Friday and they sure as shit don't involve ballot sheets, you can still tut and shake your head at people who actually are taking the time to make it to the polling stations. The people campaigning in your area? Make sure you let social media know if they were too loud, too bolshy, too unladylike, too female. You don't have to be actually voting to have an opinion, so make sure you make yours heard loud and clear! That's what this referendum is all about after all: you!

SATAN MARKS MAY 25TH ON CALENDAR

FOLLOWING the formal announcement by the government that a referendum on the repeal of the Eighth Amendment of the constitution will take place on 25 May 2018, WWN can exclusively reveal that Satan himself has eagerly marked the date in his calendar.

Carefully collating statements made by some members of the public, this publication has been able to confirm that it is highly likely that Satan is gleefully licking his lips at the thought of the Irish public possibly voting to overhaul the laws governing abortion.

'Beezlebub's nefarious and blackened soul fucking loves increasing the rights of women in the Irish constitution, the meddling, evil prick,' explained one person with knowledge of Satan's feelings on the matter. 'He's cancelled all planned torturing of sinful souls for eternity for that day too.'

'This is going to be great craic, honestly,' interrupted a booming and monstrous voice transmitted directly to our minds by Satan himself.

However, Satan is not the only entity believed to have marked the date on their calendars with the Irish public also circling the date before taking a deep, deep breath.

Elsewhere, a coven of lustful women marked the news of the referendum by burning a man alive as is in keeping with the ritualistic sacrifices they regularly perform.

GROUP THAT SOLD BABIES CRITICAL OF PEOPLE'S DECISION TO VOTE 'YES'

A GROUP which turned living, breathing children into an economic commodity by deriving profit from the illegal sale of actual children to couples in America has criticised people's decision to vote 'Yes' in the upcoming referendum, with one Bishop declaring it 'morally wrong'.

The Catholic Church, which have stated it is 'morally wrong' to vote 'Yes', forged the signatures of mothers in Mother and Baby homes so the Church could be paid for allowing walking, talking children in their care to be used in vaccine and drug trials.

It is unclear if the illegal adoptions of children in Mother and Baby homes, who were in excess of nine months old, to couples in America in exchange for cold, hard cash is considered as 'morally wrong' as voting 'Yes', due in large part to the fact the group seems unwilling to talk about the illegal adoptions. The group is similarly unsure if evidence which suggests the falsifying of death certificates could have been carried out so they could sell children illegally is as 'morally wrong' as voting 'Yes'.

The prominent organisation also aided in the concealment of the rape of children and the abetting of the priests who carried out the sexual abuse of thinking, feeling children by relocating them to other parts of the country where they continued to rape and abuse children. It is unclear whether the group thinks this is a greater 'moral wrong' than voting 'Yes'.

Some elements of the group, which is largely exempt from corporation tax, capital gains and capital acquisitions tax, have failed to pay compensation to victims of sexual abuse, often stating their displeasure at having been found financially responsible for moral wrongs not nearly as bad as voting 'Yes'.

Evidence has been found which suggests the Church, while operating the Mother and Baby home at Tuam, asked parents for money for the upkeep of some children that had already been discharged or had died. However, this same group would like you to know it is 'morally wrong' to vote 'Yes' in the upcoming referendum on the repeal of the Eighth Amendment.

'HOME TO VOTE' EXPECTED TO TURN INTO 'HOME FOR UNBELIEVABLE SESSION'

WITH the country currently heaving with Irish emigrants who have returned home to vote in the abortion referendum, craic experts have issued a level six craic warning for town centres as get-togethers break out across the land.

From countries such as Canada, America and Australia to countries such as other parts of America, Canada and Australia, expats in their thousands arrived home to Ireland this week to voice their opinion in the referendum to repeal the Eighth Amendment, driven by the 'Home to Vote' movement and a sense of solidarity with the women of Ireland.

With the voting out of the way, these thousands of mostly young men and women will now turn their attention to the most obvious course of action from this point, which is to strike up with friends they haven't seen in years and go on 'an outrageous fucking session' with no end in sight.

'They're home, they've voted… did you expect them to sit in and watch *The Late Late*?' warned senior craicologist Sean Whelan, stationed in Craicatoa, east of Ha-Ha.

'Whether they came home to vote yes or vote no, they've got like-minded people living here that have welcomed them back for the weekend, as most of them will be flying back to wherever they've made a life for themselves. So that's thousands of extra young people in Ireland for one weekend only… yeah, not many Rosaries will be said tonight, except maybe among the No side, the mad bastards.'

With 'Home to Vote' naturally evolving into 'Home For a Session', tomorrow will bring the next stage in the process, 'Home For Puking in the Kitchen Sink While Mam Gives Out'.

COMMERCE

PUBLICAN IS HIS OWN BEST CUSTOMER

FOR Waterford publican Tommy Geraghty, business at The Screaming Goat bar has been slow the last couple of years, despite his accountant reporting a 34 per cent increase volume in alcohol being sold.

'I can't make head nor tails of it,' the 59-year-old insisted, now ordering an Eastern European staff member to pull him a pint from the bottom bar as 'the runoff is better there'. 'We've gone through an extra 300 barrels

> ### 'I'm going to have to get cameras over the taps and register; someone's handing out free pints to their friends'

of the black stuff last year, yet we're actually down on revenue. Something is wrong, somewhere.'

Gulping into his lunchtime pint, Geraghty looked down past his nose, complete with a burst purple blood vessel, to the end of the glass, when a conclusion suddenly dawned on him.

'Someone's fuckin' robbing me!' he gasped, giving the barman a nod

to put on another pint. 'I'm going to have to get cameras over the taps and register; someone's handing out free pints to their friends.

'It's so hard to get decent Irish staff these days, sure you wouldn't know what these Polish lads were at over beyond.'

Mr Geraghty purchased The Screaming Goat in 2002, with the business employing hundreds of non-national workers over the years, for as little as possible per hour.

'Don't get me wrong, they're great little workers in fairness to them now,' he added, already halfway through his second pint. 'But since the wife left me in 2012, the profits have just plunged, and I guarantee you it's one of them taking advantage of the situation and fleecing me.'

Coincidentally, the grandson of four also drinks Guinness, which, according to the books, seems to be the only beer tap affected by plunging sales, followed by hundreds of missing Powers whiskey bottles.

'I'll have to keep an eye on the staff now to see who's drinking what,' Geraghty concluded, before ordering a whiskey chaser to 'settle the nerves'.

Did You Know?

Swans are capable of breaking your arm, and when in large groups they can become confident enough to slag your Ma off as well.

PARENTING

'OH, THEY WON'T BE LONG GIVING HIM BACK!' INSIST PARENTS OF ABDUCTED CHILD

THE parents of a missing child believed to have been abducted earlier today have insisted that his captors won't be long giving him back, due to his exhausting behaviour.

Geraldine and Thomas Moore reported their son Daniel, 6, missing at 2 p.m. today shortly after eyewitnesses spotted him being bundled into a white Hiace van by two men in their mid to late 30s, just metres away from the family home.

'Oh, they won't be long giving him back, let me tell you,' the boy's father said during a live television appeal, before then looking at his watch. 'It's four hours since his disappearance; he'll have them driven up the wall at this stage. The poor bastards have no idea what they've gotten themselves into.'

The Moores explained that their son, the youngest of three, is gifted at 'tormenting people', and advised his abductors to just hand him back now for their own sanity.

'He'll find some way of driving them mad,' insisted Geraldine Moore, giggling at the thought. 'Once Danny starts asking them stupid questions, that will be the end of it; they'll hand themselves in.

'He's a gas young fella, God love him; you'd want the patience of a saint.'

Gardaí have asked anyone in the Finglas area who may have seen two men driving a 09-D van this afternoon to contact Store Street Garda Station with any information.

Daniel Moore is said to be blonde, three feet one inch tall, and was last seen wearing a blue *Ben 10* T-shirt and blue stonewashed denim jeans. Daniel's parents insisted, 'just ignore his carry on' if he is found, and to hand him over to the gardaí immediately, as he can 'wreck the bulb at times.'

RURAL IRELAND TO CLOSE BY 2019

PLANS have been put in place to 'wrap up' rural Ireland by 2019, completing a 50-year-long process that has rapidly picked up pace over the last decade.

Having worked hard to decommission the rail service that linked towns and villages all over Ireland in the seventies, as well as closing dozens of garda stations over the last five years, the government is to stand back and allow An Post to shut down up to 400 post offices in rural Ireland over the next year, which will be followed by the closure of everything else over the next 18 months.

People living in rural Ireland have been advised that there will soon be 'fuck all else left for them', and that their best course of action would be to move to their nearest town before the bulldozers are sent in to scrape the countryside into the sea.

'Getting rid of rural Ireland answers so many culchie questions,' said spokesperson for the Rural Ireland Eradication Scheme, James Hennessey, 'such as "when are you going to provide a decent broadband network?" and "what are you going to do about crime in rural Ireland?" or my favourite, "how come the suicide rate in rural Ireland is so high?"

'Come 2020, those little things will all be sorted, 'cos rural Ireland is going in the friggin' bin,' he confirmed.

With rural Ireland gone, Dublin will now span over 80 per cent of the country, with areas as far as Cahirciveen in County Kerry being renamed *Dublin 764*.

LOCAL MAN OWES EVERYONE MONEY

A WATERFORD city man owes every one of his friends, family members, and unsuspecting members of the local public money, along with a long list of financial institutions, mobile phone providers, local shops, drug dealers, bars and restaurants, WWN can confirm.

James Crook, 36, who somehow manages to never have money despite holding down a full-time job, was unavailable for comment today as his phone was going straight to messenger, with a recorded message pointing out that the voicemail was full and to try again later.

'Yup, that's our Jimbo alright – always has the phone off on payday,' explained long-time friend Ger Clancy, who admitted to not knowing exactly why he was still friends with Crook as he owes him €500 for the past four years. 'If you do manage to catch him, will you tell him to give me a shout straight away? Oh, and Martin, Tracey, Tom, Karl,

Colm too. Actually, just forget about it; you'll have a better chance of catching Ebola.

'That cunt is probably in a pub somewhere spending his wages before anyone can ask him for their money back,' he added.

In a bid to track down Crook, WWN visited several local bars in the area of his home, many with owners also asking for the elusive grandson of four to 'give them a shout'.

'Fucker has a tab here since 2007,' one publican explained. 'Every time I see him, he says that he's "waiting on a claim to come through", or that there was a "mix up at the bank and he didn't get paid" – you can always tell when the little bollocks is lying.'

Sources on the ground later confirmed that Crook was spotted outside a city centre chipper, asking people for a lend of €5 for a kebab tray, before pulling out his iPhone 8 and ordering a taxi home.

More as we get it.

PATHETIC STUDENT DOESN'T EVEN HAVE CHLAMYDIA YET

WATERFORD native Marcus Phelan is continuing to waste the best years of his life by studying and attending lectures, with sources close to the 18-year-old confirming that he hasn't even picked up a sexually transmitted disease yet.

Phelan, currently living in Dublin where he attends UCD, is said to be 100 per cent disease and infection free, after sleeping with only one girl since moving to the city, and taking the correct safety precautions such as wearing a condom like a big sad virgin would do.

With his penis free from discharge and his urine free from white mucus-y particles that sting him when he pees, Phelan continues to excel in his engineering course, giving his fellow students plenty to mock him about.

'Ha, look at him over

there, not hungover, not frantically scratching the tip of his penis,' said Phelan's classmate Mark Gennon, frantically scratching the tip of his penis.

'How is that the college experience? You're young, you're away from home for the first time, you have fuck all money so you just get wrecked on cheap wine and have bareback sex because you can't afford rubbers. Here's this chump over here, not even a wart on his tool, making the rest of us look like we're idiots or something. Is peer pressure not a thing now that we've made the switch from secondary school to college? What the fuck is going on?'

Reports are also coming in that Phelan has yet to try drugs of any kind, which has bumped him from the category of 'sad bastard' to 'fucking pure sad bastard altogether'.

MOTORING

NEW D-PLATES WILL HELP IDENTIFY DICKHEADS ON THE ROAD

FOLLOWING the success of the N-plates for novice drivers on our roads in recent years, the Motoring Commission of Ireland is set to introduce new D-plates to help road users to ascertain which cars around them are being driven by total dickheads.

The D-plates will be mandatory for any driver who has accrued more than six penalty points for persistent speeding in 12 months, any driver who uses the excuse, 'sure I only had two or three pints' when breathalysed, and any driver who uses their mobile phone to take a selfie or send a video while behind the wheel of a car.

In the instance of the latter condition, special powers are being granted to traffic cops to issue penalties to selfie-posting drivers even if they don't catch them on the road, with the garda Snapchat division

> **'It's amazing to think that we as motorists have been sharing the road with total arseholes for a long time'**

already seeking out offenders on the social media platform.

Unlike the N-plate, which drivers must carry for 24 months, the new D-plate will be permanent, with traffic cops stating that 'once a dickhead, always a dickhead'.

'It's amazing to think that we as motorists have been sharing the road with total arseholes for a long time,' said a spokesperson for the Department of Transport.

'You might be obeying the rules of the road, but the guy two lanes

across from you might be recording his own sketch comedy video for his 37 followers on Twitter, talking pure shite and not watching the road. So, a D-plate will allow other motorists to say, 'Okay, that lad is clearly a fucking dose. Let's just give him a wide berth so that when he loses control and rams into a tree, at least he doesn't clip us.'

It is expected that by 2021 there will be a sum total of 27 cars in Ireland not brandishing a D-plate.

Wonderful World of Science

Can exposing children to the internet at a young age harm them? Researchers at UCD are set to show a group of toddlers an ISIS beheading video to find out!

LANGUAGE

CULCHIE DOESN'T UNDERSTAND HALF THE THINGS HE COMES OUT WITH

'One of the lads asked me how the weekend was, and I think I said something along the lines of, "Arra sure you know yourself, when the owl is in the hen house sure the tay won't scald you"'

DYED-in-the-wool countryman Ian McClennon has admitted to WWN that he 'doesn't understand half of the culchie bullshit' he comes out with on a daily basis, in an emotional exclusive interview.

McClennon, 28, is originally from the midlands but moved to Dublin earlier this year, where he now works in IT for a prominent accountancy company, alongside hundreds of native Dubliners and 'a few foreign lads too'.

Eager to stay true to his culchie roots, McClennon confided to WWN that he sometimes plays up his natural midlands accent, and has also dropped numerous 'culchie sayings' into everyday conversation that make absolutely no sense, some of which he has made up on the spot in the middle of conversations when he has completely run out of anything else to say.

'One of the lads asked me how the weekend was, and I think I said something along the lines of, "Arra sure you know yourself, when the owl is in the hen house sure the tay won't scald you,"' sobbed McClennon, his eyes wet with tears.

'Like, what in the fuck does that even mean? I think it's a self-defence thing, these Dubs always look at me like I'm the token bogger anyways so I just play that up instead of telling them to fuck off. They seem to be humoured by that kind of shit, so I'll keep it coming, but I'll try and make at least some of it even slightly intelligible.'

McClennon cut his interview short after a co-worker asked him if he'd like to go for a pint later that evening, to which the midlander replied, 'Would a 1987 Ford Cortina like a Prius to rear-end it on the M50?'

LOCAL CHEF RUNNING OUT OF PLACES TO WORK

A COUNTY Waterford man is currently running out of places to work after once again walking out of another head chef job at a local gastropub, WWN has learned.

Mark Doran, who has been cheffing for the last 16 years, stormed out of Joxer's Inn on Sunday morning after having an altercation with publican David Hayes, who confronted the hungover 38-year-old over his attitude towards staff and his propensity to give out stink when a meal is returned by a customer.

'Anytime someone wasn't happy with his food he'd throw a strop, like he was after cooking some Michelin star dish,' one staff member explained, who admitted to being glad to see the back of the 'miserable cunt'. 'Like, he was mostly making burgers and chicken wings, stuff a 10-year-old could cook, yet still managed to fuck it up while acting like one.

'He was only working here a wet week and he's already gone; that's the 10th head chef we've had in two years,' he added. 'They're all so sensitive.'

Speaking to WWN, Mr Doran pointed to poor management skills for leaving his latest role, but confirmed he has already secured another cheffing job in another pub down the road.

'This is basically my last option now as I've worked in every bar and restaurant in the city at this stage,' he admitted. 'If this doesn't work out I'll probably have to relocate to another city and start afresh, or maybe address my anger management issues, but where's the fun in that, right?'

UPDATE: Mark Doran has since left his new role over 'creative differences' and the fact that 'everyone is shit except for him'.

TEENAGER ONLY SPEAKS IN GIFS NOW

WATERFORD teen Petey Willins has begun what may very well be a lifelong vow of silence, after deciding to speak purely in the form of GIFs – short looping images with a funny line of text running underneath – from now on.

GIFs, sometimes pronounced GIFs, have become hugely popular in recent years with the rise of app-based communication such as WhatsApp, Facebook Messenger and Snapchat. The usually humorous snippets of movies, TV shows, sporting occasions and random shite now form the basis of all conversation, with skilled users able to carry entire conversations without uttering a single word.

Willins, 16, is believed to be the first person in the world to forgo the spoken word in favour of cat videos and clips from episodes of *Archer*, and was delighted when we told him that he had entered history as a pioneer in the evolution of language.

'SpongeBob jumping into a hole and covering himself over,' was displayed on the iPad that Willins wears around his neck, with a translator helping us decipher that the youth was so amazed at what was happening, he literally felt like dying and burying himself.

'Did you have any idea that what you were doing was so groundbreaking?', we asked.

'A black man looking smugly to camera and tapping the side of his head,' displayed the iPad, with our translator stating that Willins was saying that he was very smart, and perhaps smarter than anyone else.

'Fuck this,' WWN concluded, and left the youth to it.

Parish Notes

The funeral of Edith O'Donnell, hairdresser and inventor of the fringe will take place this week.

EXCLUSIVE

'I DON'T KNOW HOW, BUT THIS PINT GLASS IS COMING HOME WITH ME'

'IF you're asking me why I've suddenly turned this simple, normal night out into *Ocean's 11*, then I don't have an answer for you,' said Peter Cannaghan, his eyes never moving from the pint glass in front of him, still containing at least half of his pint of Hop To It, a new craft lager that the barman in the Crowing Donkey had just served him.

'But all I can tell you is this. I don't know how, but that pint glass is coming home with me this night. It's going to take every single one of my pint glass robbing skills, skills that I have not used since I was a student,

but mark my words: I'm drinking my orange juice out of that thing in the morning.'

Cannaghan, 38, knew he wanted the pint glass the moment he saw it, his mind filling with a desire that he hadn't known since the first time he saw the sweet Guinness pint glass with the swirl that ran from top to bottom, or the very first widget-enabled Harp glasses in the late nineties.

With his mind set on robbing the glass to rebuild his collection once again after it was massacred by his wife Lena when they moved house, Cannaghan spent the last half hour ignoring what his friends had been chatting about, opting instead to 'scope out the bar' for possible exits, keeping an eye on the bar staff to make sure they didn't notice the glass missing,

and being extremely vigilant so that the lounge boy doesn't lift it off the table when Cannaghan nips out for a slash.

'Why the fuck did I wear the little jacket tonight?' Cannaghan cursed himself, imagining how much easier this whole heist would be if he was wearing his winter jacket with the deep pockets.

'If only I could convince Lena to put it in her handbag when we're going, but she'd freak out. I can hear her now, "Oh, what do we want a dirty pint glass in the house for, they don't even fit in the dishwasher…" Are you kidding me? Look at the thing! It's got textured hops running up the side of it! It's got the logo embossed in dark emerald! It's the coolest pint glass I've ever seen. It's going up my shirt and out the door, if it kills me.'

UPDATE: When last we heard from Mr Cannaghan, he had successfully managed to tuck the pint glass under his arm and smuggle it out of the pub by draping his jacket over his shoulder, but unfortunately let it drop and smash when he waved for a taxi.

LOCAL MAN'S BANK BALANCE DROPS BY EIGHTEEN PINTS

THERE was economic chaos for Dermot Creland at the start of business today after his bank balance dropped sharply by eighteen pints, the worst weekend trading result in history for the Dublin man.

Creland's account had looked in good shape yesterday evening, but a series of payments to vintners, publicans and off-licensed premises took effect after the close of business last night, wiping the value of eighteen pints of Heineken off his shares in one fell swoop, sending the Creland house into uproar.

The sharp drop is said to be a result of a failure to act according to external stimulus over the weekend, with Creland making a series of poor choices after listening to shaky advice from his close financial advisors, namely 'Wee Eoin Up The Road' and 'Cuntface Derek'.

With little to no memory of what happened on Saturday night in town, Dermot was pleased to see his online balance was still healthy on Monday morning, and was therefore distraught when he noticed that DC's value had suffered such heavy losses.

'We're looking at ways we can rebuild his economy, before sanctions are put in place to stop this kind of thing happening again,' said Dermot's wife, Maire Creland, brought in to help sort out the mess.

'We've had multi-pint drops in the past, but this is beyond reckoning. There hasn't been a day this bad for the DC since he went to his cousin's wedding in 2004, a day which still lives in our memory as "Black Saturday". I've put some calming measures in place to help things settle here, and then there'll be some extreme financial regulations imposed, as well as a ban on dealing with those pricks up the road who take him out on these fucking benders.'

Creland has pleaded with the central bank of his wife for some sort of bailout program, but so far his application has been unsuccessful.

SUICIDAL DUBLIN MAN BUYS BICYCLE

THE family and friends of a Dublin man have expressed concerns over his state of mind and mental wellbeing, after he announced that he will be commuting to work through the city by bicycle from now on.

Patrick Donaghan, who lives in Inchicore but commutes every day to the IFSC, showed off his new bike to his friends at the weekend, immediately sparking fears that he was about to do something regrettable such as attempt to cycle up the quays twice a day in rush-hour traffic.

With cycling in Dublin becoming hazardous to the point of being completely lethal, an intervention is being staged for Donaghan by his friends to remind him that there are people who care about him very much, and even if life sometimes seems tough, there are always options open to him that don't involve trying to hold his own on a bicycle against the cruel, uncaring Dublin traffic.

'Like a lot of tragic cases in our country, Patrick seems happy and healthy, but obviously there's a hidden darkness in there,' sobbed a close friend of the cyclist.

'And we can't just sit by and say "yeah, he's fine". He obviously isn't. We want to just get him to open up to us, to talk to us, to let him know that maybe one of us is driving past the IFSC in the mornings and if he meets us at Heuston, we'll drop him up the road. We just don't want to sit back and do nothing, and then hear that something dreadful has happened.'

If you have a friend who may be in danger of cycling in Dublin city centre or indeed anywhere else in the country where drivers don't account for cyclists, WWN urges you to have a word with them before it's too late.

LITERATURE

LOCAL MAN REREADS CHAPTER IN BOOK FOR SECOND TIME AFTER MIND WANDERS OFF

DESPITE getting three pages in, Waterford man Patrick Lyons was forced to restart the chapter in his latest book reading endeavour after his mind just wandered off of its own accord, WWN can confirm.

Rereading the words he had already apparently read, but somehow failed to process, the 34-year-old restarted chapter four in another attempt, this time vowing to concentrate solely on the book's content.

'How did I continue physically reading the pages and yet still manage to veer off in a daydream,' Lyons asked himself, unaware he was now doing the exact same thing again. 'My finger seems to be scrolling through the text and turning the pages, but I'm off in my own little world thinking about stupid things and not soaking any of the material in.

'Ah, fuck! I'm after doing it again!' he realised, restarting the same chapter for the second time in ten minutes. 'Argh, stop it! Stop it!'

'Maybe I'm some kind of prodigy that can read and think about something totally different at the same time,' he then posed, before coming to the conclusion that he literally has no idea what he just read.

'I just want to read my book in peace with no distractions,' he shouted at his mind in the hope that some part of it would listen to his request.

'Shit, maybe I've undiagnosed ADHD,' he then concluded, before throwing his book into the nearest bin.

The Solution Zone!

Noting the dire state the world is in today, WWN proposes practical solutions to some of Ireland's and the world's most pressing issues.

O'Connell Street:

– O'Connell Street has become one of the most dangerous streets in Ireland. Be sure to take your selfies from a distance. Bonus – you get the whole Spire in the shot.

– The British army in 1916 were able to approach O'Connell Street using modified delivery trucks which doubled as armoured cards. Maybe give that a go?

– You can still see the bullet holes from the rising in the columns of the GPO. Just make sure you're not looking at the bullet holes from a more recent shooting. Make sure you're looking at the right ones!

– If you find yourself in Dublin after a night out, remember that O'Connell Street has everything you need. Fast-food restaurants, plenty of public transport options, large amounts of knife crime, and one guard. His name is Seán! Say hello!

– Experts have suggested that O'Connell Street should be nuked from orbit, adding that 'it's the only way to be sure'.

– In order to clean up O'Connell St we propose a weapon amnesty. This means anyone who has a weapon can hand it into gardaí without being arrested. Similarly, local businesses will be offered a 'neon sign amnesty' whereby they can help rid the street of garish shop signage that plagues O'Connell Street.

– Is O'Connell Street Bridge part of O'Connell Street? Answers to WWN HQ please.

– We propose a shortening of O'Connell Street by some 30 metres, meaning that when the St Patrick's Day parade rolls around, US marching bands will have 30 metres less ground to march on while torturing the public with their awful fucking music.

– People have complained that the rich history and architecture of O'Connell Street is under threat, and we at WWN agree which is why we demand Dr Quirkey's Good Time Emporium be listed as an official national treasure and UNESCO World Heritage Site.

– Nelson's Pillar was famously blown up on the street in 1966. WWN proposes an annual, commemorative explosion to mark the famous event and we volunteer the Spire as the first monument to be used in the celebratory explosion.

IN-DEPTH REPORT

'WE'VE LIVED HERE FOR 40 YEARS': LIFE IN IRELAND AS A BLOW-IN

THE most recent census has highlighted an oft-ignored section of the Irish population who suffer in silence every day, simply for living in an area where they were not born. As part of WWN's ongoing 'Life In Ireland' series, today we delve into the sad, lonely existence of the blow-in.

Blow-ins make up almost 90 per cent of the population of Ireland, with very few people actually still living in their place of birth. Most people migrate to neighbouring towns or further afield due to a number of reasons such as lack of jobs, marital status, or hating the sight of everyone in their home town.

Upon arrival in their new home, these people are immediately stamped with the 'blow-in' label and ostracised from the rest of the community, with many finding the label to be utterly permanent.

'We moved to Carrickavannagh from Dublin in early 1976, but they still call us "the Dubs",' sobbed Margaret McFerrin, speaking

exclusively to WWN on National Blow-In Day, which was put together by the Blow-In Association of Ireland to help blow-ins all across the country.

'My husband Padraig served as a guard here for 30 years. I was on the school committee on a voluntary basis for 20 years. I clean the fucking church every Sunday after mass, on my own time. We're both on the Tidy Towns. But no, to the people of Carrickavannagh, we're just blow-ins that came down in the last shower.'

Across Ireland, most blow-ins are treated just like any other part of the community while in the company of their neighbours, but dismissed as 'fly-by-nights' once their back is turned, with many looked down on as being 'as bad as the foreigners' and 'more

than likely some sort of drug dealer', something which a spokesperson for the BIAI wishes to address.

'In Ireland, there are over four million blow-ins silently suffering every day,' said Margaret Harrison, a Brit who moved here ten years ago.

'These people are ostracised from their communities, and segregated from essential services such as the craic after mass and pints after the under-21 team wins some local championship. And for what? For being among the people who decided to move to somewhere more than ten minutes away from where they were born.'

If you are a blow-in and this article has affected you, then please fuck off back to whatever town you came from.

45

MILK NICER OUT OF CUPS, INSIST CULCHIES

THE National Culchie Association of Ireland (NCAI) has published its annual report into things it likes, with milk tasting better in cups being their number one favourite.

Speaking at Dublin Castle today, and for no apparent reason, chairman Paddy Cooney listed off an array of different things that rural Irish people voted for in 2017, including Tayto crisp and brown sauce sandwiches, buttered digestives, biting the caramel top off of Mars bars before eating the nugget base, red lead blaas, Nathan Carter and comedian Neil Delamere.

'We are proud to announce that the majority of culchies prefer to drink milk out of cups, as opposed to glasses,' Mr Cooney addressed the emotional audience, many of whom travelled vast distances to attend the AGM today.

Following a lengthy standing ovation and several 'Hip, hip, hoorays', stewards at the venue distributed cups of milk to everyone before a toast was raised by the chairman.

'For years, rural men and women have been lambasted for opting for a mug of milk, but no more shall we hide, no more shall we hang our heads in shame to the city folk, for we are united as one!' Cooney toasted, now wiping a tear from his cheek and milk moustache from his nicotine-stained upper lip.

Today's announcement is set to change the way city restaurants deal with strange culchie menu requests.

'We've even started to stock pigs' feet, or trotters as the boggers call them,' one Camden Street establishment told WWN. 'Despite having different tastes, I suppose they're people too and as a food business we need to address their needs.'

The restaurant has already included a cup of milk option on their lunch and evening menu.

'It's priced at €3.99, but it's organic and unpasteurised, just how culchies like it.'

FRESH reports have confirmed that local council worker Mark Shevlin is 'this close' to complaining to his foreman about how he always gets stuck on 'Stop/Go' duty, and never gets a turn on the little Hi-Mac digger thing instead.

Now on his fourth year with Waterford County Council, Shevlin spoke exclusively to WWN about 'having an arseful' with his job, due to being constantly relegated to lollipop work while the rest of his team of workmates get to do all the 'cool shit', like drive miniature plant equipment and sit in the van all day reading *The Sun*.

Shevlin, 33, is otherwise happy with the pay and conditions that he

COUNCIL WORKER NEVER GETS TURN ON THE LITTLE DIGGER

receives for his efforts, but stressed that if he gets put on traffic control one more time, there's a very real chance that he'll 'lose his shit'.

'There's Keith on the Bobcat again – that's his fifth go this month,' griped Shevlin, deliberately letting a queue of traffic sit there for 90 seconds longer than necessary out of pure spite.

'I never get a go, it's not fair. Let one of those bastards come out here and spin this bitch of a thing for a change, and let me into the cab of that digger where it's nice and warm.

'And don't start on about that under-qualified shite, we're not actually digging anything; we just kinda paw at the road for a day and then piss off.'

UPDATE: Shevlin has absconded in a miniature backhoe, and is said to be making his way through Waterford city centre at speeds of up to 8 km/h.

FUCKING BANKLINK ONLY GIVES FIFTIES

WATERFORD residents down to the last €30 in their accounts before payday have been warned that the banklink on Meagher's Quay only has €50 notes, and is liable to catch you out when you badly need to withdraw a twenty.

Locals were first made aware of the, 'withdrawals in multiples of €50 only' predicament after hearing the anguished sobs of foiled revellers last night, who discovered all too late that they were not able to get their last twenty quid out for chips while on their way out of the pubs in town.

With not even a shop open to allow them to get a pack of chewing gum and €10 cashback, dozens of Waterford pissheads were forced to do without a kebab and no option but to mournfully walk home, with not one taxi in the city having a 'pay by laser' option.

'There should be a law that states that the closer we get to payday, the lower the denomination of notes in ATMs, said Cllr Luke Kernahan, who found himself walking home after a mad one last night.

'First week after payday, have all the fifties you want. Week two and three, then you really need €20 notes and even tenners, tops. That last week before your next paycheque comes in? That's when ATMs want to start dropping spare change into a little cup like at the self-service checkout, so if all you have to your name is €7.80, you can get it out.'

The matter is to be discussed at this week's council meeting, as well as the matter of shops that won't give you cashback on purchases of less than €5, useless if all you have is €3.75.

GERRY ADAMS ANNOUNCES NEW ROLE AS AMNESIA IRELAND SPOKESPERSON

AFTER he announced his decision to step down as Sinn Féin president in 2018, much speculation has been devoted to what was in store next for Ireland's political saviour Gerry Adams. That speculation can now come to an end, as he has been confirmed as the spokesperson for Amnesia Ireland.

'We were searching for a high-profile person who could talk of the devastating effects amnesia can have and who better than Gerry,' explained a spokesperson for the charity and awareness-raising group.

'Normal, everyday people might know what it's like to forget where you parked your car in a shopping centre car park, but Gerry can help people understand what it's like to have absolutely no recollection of conversations with IRA victims, abuse victims and the family members of both abuse victims and the disappeared,' the spokesperson added.

While up to this point Adams, who had denied intentions to become a full-time meme post-Sinn Féin presidency, has never spoken of his struggles with amnesia, it is hoped in his post-politics life his struggles can help others cope.

'We're talking about possibly the world's most high-profile convenient "forgetterer" of crucially important

information. If people don't hate amnesia and want to cure it after hearing how Gerry can't remember anything of importance, then I don't think there's an alternative that can work,' concluded the spokesperson.

In a brief statement delivered after announcing he would step down as leader of Sinn Féin, Adams spoke of his condition.

'It may be Amnesia Ireland's recollection of events that I am to become their ambassador, but I do not recall such a conversation, on any such day in the future, past or present that they may come to mention. It's simply untrue,' Adams confirmed before further softening everyone's impression of him with another tweet.

Parish Notes

A meeting of the Camouflage Enthusiasts' Club on the quays has been cancelled yet again as members failed to show up.

PARENTING

HOUSEWIDE PANIC AS LOCAL MOTHER THREATENS TO COUNT TO THREE

THERE have been reports of small children darting around a Waterford household in a fit of panic after one mother in her early 30s threatened to count to three.

Previously content with 'acting the complete bollocks', Martin, 8, Aine,

6, and Brian, 4, all children belonging to Rachel Clancey, are now said to be rushing around looking for a place to hide after the threat was issued by their mother.

'Shit, shit, shit,' confirmed Martin, who had no idea his mother would react so harshly to him pouring a bag of flour on the kitchen floor and using his younger brother as a mop in a bid to clean up the mess.

Rachel, who was only upstairs for two minutes, delivered the threat which sent shivers up her children's spines despite being aware of how it could serve to terrorise her children.

'Uh, oh,' added Aine, who maintained she has no idea how her glitter pens ended up all over the wallpaper under the stairs, all while she fled the scene to the safety of her bedroom where she planned on pretending to be asleep despite it only being 4.46 p.m.

The uneasy truce between mother and children was broken thanks to the children 'acting like little shits'. However, Rachel still hasn't made good on following through with the threat and commencing the dreaded count to three.

More as we get it.

LOCAL MAN JUST COVERS UNFLUSHED POO WITH BIT OF TISSUE

IN the cold white porcelain of a Waterford toilet, a small turd lay in a shallow pool of water, three squares of two-ply Kittensoft barely covering its tiny brown body.

Detective Malcolm Decker had heard about cases like this before, but this was the first time he'd witnessed one for himself.

'I've worked these streets for years, but sometimes there's a case that will still shock me,' said Decker, lighting one e-cig off another.

'What we have here is a turd, probably arrived into this world with his friends. Then they all get flushed, but this poor bastard gets separated. Who knows why. Maybe the flush on the toilet wasn't strong enough, maybe our turd just had too much bran. Either way, he doesn't go down the bend like his pals.'

Decker paused to let the forensic team pass by, as a crime scene photographer lit up the downstairs loo with eerie flashbulb pops from a high-powered polaroid camera.

'So our turd in the bowl now probably thinks that he's going to get a second hit

of the flush, right? One more flush, and he's gone,' Decker continued, the stubble on his face showing that he had been up for almost 36 hours on this case.

'But, no, whoever was doing the flushing, he didn't bother to do the right thing. He didn't bother to wait 60 seconds for the cistern to fill, didn't bother to give this poor shit any kind of special treatment. No, he just covered it up. Covered it with a few sheets of toilet paper, and then just walked away as if everything was okay. Like everything was just, fucking fine! Well, things aren't fine. And I'm going to catch this bastard if it god damn kills me, because 20 years on the force has taught me one thing: the kind of person that would cover an unflushed turd with toilet paper and walk away once, well, that's the kind of person who would do it again.'

Decker and his team finished their crime scene investigations and left the Waterford house, walking past the family who live there, paying particular attention to the father of the house who seemed to be acting very suspiciously.

'That's the guy,' Decker mumbled to himself as he left. 'That's our fucking guy.'

EXCLUSIVE

REMEMBERING TRAGIC WINTER SOLSTICE '89

FOR many, the winter solstice is the perfect time of year to come together in pagan worship, as the first sun of the shortest day of the year cracks across the Boyne horizon and showers Newgrange with light. But for some, the wounds of 21 December, 1989 still run too deep.

It started like any other winter solstice – 99.9 per cent of the population still in bed, with only the true die-hard onlookers assembling at the ancient burial mound at Newgrange to see the dawn light stream through the chambers.

Officials at the site knew something was wrong when complaints began to rumble from the people at the far end of the chamber, growing angry that they were 'stood behind some big fat bastard'. The situation grew worse when said fat bastard emitted 'the worst fart in the history of the Boyne Valley', sparking a huge panic which resulted in the 47 people in the chamber

completely missing the sunlight as it entered the chamber, blinded with the stink.

Although the people in the chamber still had a chance to escape at this point, local historian Darrach Guinan tells WWN that the ghosts of the druids had other plans.

'You don't rock up to an ancient burial ground and shite your kecks,' said Guinan, at an unveiling of a plaque to mark the 28th anniversary of the tragedy.

'While everyone was kicking off the druids emerged from their ancient

> ### 'You don't rock up to an ancient burial ground and shite your kecks'

slumber and started crawling out of the walls, feasting on the flesh of the helpless solstice watchers. I was just a boy outside the chamber, but I'll never forget the sound of the druids as they munched on bones. Then one druid came to the front, merely a skeleton with rags hanging from his bones. He told us all to fuck off and went back inside.'

Tickets have gone on sale for Solstice '19, and are already trading hands for thousands of euro on DoneDeal.

Suburban Dictionary

'Donkey's years' – a unit of time first discovered by a farmer who claimed he could communicate with donkeys, who told him one single donkey year equated to a decade of human time.

BREAKING NEWS

COMPANY MOVES ONLY NON-CAUCASIAN EMPLOYEE TO CENTRE OF EVERY PROMOTIONAL PHOTO

A PROGRESSIVE Dublin-based business consulting firm has ensured its only non-Caucasian employee, Joshua Varané, takes centre stage in every team photo featuring in their soon-to-be published company brochure.

Believed to be related to reasons entirely to do with the fact that he is mixed race, and that this reflects well on his employers somehow, Varané has been marshalled to key positions in countless photos, but not in an obvious way that makes it clear just what management at Cliff Edge Solutions are playing at.

'I'm being fucked right into the middle of these photos because I'm black, amn't I?' Varané asked a colleague after the company's CEO

Health and Well-being Tip

If you don't have anxiety, don't worry; you will once you read the 400 articles online about how you might actually have it.

shouted 'you' and gestured Varané towards the empty space next to him in the front row of a group of chairs.

Varané smiled politely while becoming increasingly frustrated, with the slightest suspicion that he had unwittingly been placed in some sort of sequel to the movie *Get Out* slowly creeping into his mind.

Thanks to the presence of Varané in the every photo in the company brochure, management at Cliff Edge Solutions will feel emboldened to instruct PR firms to make note of how the company is 'diverse, progressive, diverse again, and reflective of modern Ireland'.

Just when Varané didn't think he could more excluded and marginalised, he was informed his winning smile had made it onto the homepage of the company's website.

WHILE some people are sideswiped by a mid-life crisis that comes from out of nowhere, Waterford man Cathal Passerton has a fair idea about when his will hit, what he's going to do, and how it will affect those in his life, thanks to an excellent planning process that began when he hit 35.

Now 39, Passerton has made sure that he's working in a dead-end job that he's completely bored of, as well as welcoming the birth of his third child just when he and his wife Susan were settling back into some semblance of a routine after their first two kids.

Now with just enough money to either look after his family to a comfortable degree or opt instead to buy himself the motorbike that he always wanted but could never afford, Passerton is 'all set' for a rocky,

'I just can't help but feel that I'm missing out on some great opportunities to embarrass myself in front of all our friends'

LOCAL MAN LAYING GROUNDWORK FOR PRETTY EPIC MID-LIFE CRISIS

tumultuous next five years, and has already rehearsed a few screaming arguments with his wife about how he feels that he has wasted his potential and just wants more from life, dammit.

'I don't blame my wife and kids for the fact that I lead a boring life where nothing changes and I never have enough money to do the things I've always wanted to do. But actually, yeah, I do blame them,' said the Dungarvan native, shopping for clothes that would generally look better on a man ten years younger.

'I just can't help but feel that I'm missing out on some great opportunities to embarrass myself in front of all our friends, to be "that guy" – the guy who is the oldest man in the nightclub, the guy who thinks he's still attractive to sexy young women even though he's carrying a lot of weight

and looking rougher than he's ever looked. Maybe I'll get a tattoo. Maybe I'll sniff some cocaine, see what that's like. It'll all work out in the best, most dreadful way.'

Passerton confirmed that he also thinks he 'has a shot' at an affair with a girl from work, despite how cliched that may sound.

SKYSCRAPER IN THE SHAPE OF MICHAEL COLLINS GETS GO AHEAD IN CORK

AN entirely uncontroversial proposal to build a skyscraper in the shape of Michael Collins was given the green light in Cork before any formal planning permission was even submitted.

The reception the county has given the proposed skyscraper, set for Cork city's docklands, sits in stark contrast to other proposals for multi-storey buildings, around which a swell of opposition has been steadily growing.

'Class!' the county of Cork said in response to the proposed 170-storey Collins-scraper, cutting off the building's designer mid-sentence despite his probably having more key information to divulge.

'Shush, shush, shush, we'll stop you there, boy, you had us at Michael Collins,' added Cork, already beaming with pride

at the mere thoughts of what a glorious beacon the building could become.

The skyscraper, which will be built entirely out of discarded materials and waste from a disused nuclear power plant, and see Collins naked from the waste down, has been allowed bypass all the usual planning procedures, such is the enthusiasm for the project.

'Obviously, we here in the Rebel County are in no way prone to becoming overexcited, so we've taken every precaution necessary to ensure no lads from Dublin will be allowed partake in the construction,' said one Cork City planning official, who dislocated his shoulder after repeatedly slamming an 'accepted' stamp on a page solely containing the words 'Michael Collins skyscraper'.

COMMUTE BEST PART OF MAN'S DAY

LOCAL man Phillip Drimlon has hit back at claims that his 90-minute commute in and out of Dublin city centre 'must be hell', before firmly stating that having three hours each day to himself is the only thing that keeps him going.

Having purchased a house 'within commuting distance' to Dublin in the height of the boom, father of four Drimlon has spent the better part of the last decade perfecting his get-to-work game, and has his system of bus, train and Luas transfers down to a fine art.

Although most of his friends and co-workers consider him to be mental for undertaking such a lengthy trek to and from work each day, Drimlon states that the combination of having no supervisors chasing him for work and no kids screaming at him for no particular reason has

made the journey 'the best part of his day'.

'Ok, so you think the 90 minutes I have each morning to listen to podcasts, read books and watch box sets on my phone are the worst part of my day?' smiled Drimlon, who doesn't even mind not getting a seat most days.

'I'm here with my headphones in, chilling out, taking in the scenery. It's bliss. When I get to work, that's when shit kicks off. Then when I get home, it's a tornado of getting the kids to bed before I pan out myself. But getting there and back? Even if there's a smell of day-old piss coming from the leaky toilet on the train, it's still a joy.'

UPDATE: Drimlon's blissful commute has been shattered by a co-worker who now shares the train with him, resulting in an hour of pointless work based chit-chat and banal small talk each way.

EXCLUSIVE

LOCAL WOMAN THINKS SHE'S SASSY, BLESS HER

MISTAKING unfriendliness for personality, Waterford local Una McNiall is currently halfway through alienating herself from her friends, family and co-workers, with the charmless 23-year-old dismissing these people as 'unable to handle her'.

McNiall began to embrace her inner geebag after leaving college last year, after deciding that being nice to people and not ending every conversation with a bitchy put-down didn't sit with her edgy, cool new persona.

From being overly rude to waiting staff and taxi drivers to putting down the ideas and suggestions of co-workers during meetings, the Tramore native spent the last year being really smugly happy with how quick-witted she is, completely missing the mortified looks of everyone around her.

Under the impression that she's being sassy and that everyone thinks she's really badass and cool, McNiall's contact with her closest friends has dropped off sharply in recent weeks, causing her to dismiss her former pals with a snappy line that she read on the internet somewhere.

'If you can't handle me at my worst, you don't deserve me at my best,' quipped McNiall on Facebook, a pointed jab at people who have already unfriended her and therefore will never see it.

'But, like, if any of you want to do something at the weekend, I'm free, okay? I've had a lot of cancellations lately, people not answering my phone calls or WhatsApps. Maybe it's because they can't handle my sassiness, I don't know. Maybe I should be more sassy? Turn up the sass? Look up sass in a dictionary to make sure I'm doing it right?'

McNiall then went looking through her favourite meme pages to see if there was a passive aggressive post about former friends that summed up exactly how she feels so that she could retweet it with the caption 'You know who you all are'.

LOCAL MAN STILL LICKS INSIDE OF CRISP BAG

WATERFORD local and 100 per cent fully grown adult Derek Leeson has come out and admitted that although it's the kind of thing that he would chastise his small children for, he still licks the last crumbs out of every bag of crisps he buys.

After years of trying to convince his wife that he was just 'tearing the bags up for the bin', Leeson held a press conference attended by 19 delegates from WWN, where he unrepentantly discussed his love of getting the absolute most out of his crisps, by employing bag-licking techniques that he learned as a child.

Taking us through a 47-slide PowerPoint presentation on the matter, Leeson described how his now 38-year-old fingers are too big to get the last, tastiest grains of salt and flavour from the corners of his crisp bags, and how tearing the bag open is the only course of action if you want those delicious crumbs.

'You can dredge the bag with a licked finger all you want, there are some crumbs that will not come out until you get licking,' said a proud Leeson, as his wife Lorraine cried tears of embarrassment beside him.

'Split the bag down the side, flatten it out, and then get ready for flavour town. And before you all judge, let me ask you this, what would you have me otherwise do? Throw out a bag of crisps that still had yummy crumbs in it? Those are the best bit! You're all so busy being mature and polite, you've forgotten the sheer joy of a hit of pure smushed up barbecue Hula Hoops.'

Mr Leeson immediately set about demonstrating his method, before being served with divorce papers by his wife.

TRAVEL NEWS

WATERFORD MAN NOT SURE IF YOU ARE AWARE, BUT HE'S LIVING IN NEW YORK AT THE MOMENT

A WATERFORD man, currently living in New York, has expressed his considerable worry at the possibility that you might not know he's actually living in New York at the minute, WWN can confirm.

Cathal Frelihy, original from Dungarvan, has been in the Big Apple since October and although he is enjoying his new digs and surroundings, he is fearful a few people may still be unaware of this fact.

Frelihy had gone on an extensive farewell tour of Waterford to inform anyone who was within earshot that he was off to New York, but remains unsure people knew that such conversations meant he was, actually, going, to New York like.

'I'm due back for good in May next year and if there's still a few people who had no idea I was over here, you'd start to question if it was worth it at all'

'I mean you can update Instagram with selfies 15-20 times a day, you can have endless Snapchat stories, but it's always in the back of your mind, "what if that lad I was in primary school with years ago doesn't know

I'm living it up in New York? Or that girl I worked with in the bar over the summer seven years ago?" That stuff haunts you boi,' Frelihy explained to WWN.

Despite Facebook status updates in the hundreds, all featuring pictures of Frelihy in New York, the 26-year-old confessed to being sick with worry that some poor unfortunates had no idea how he was in *the* New York city.

'Sure word gets around, but I'm due back for good in May next year and if there's still a few people who had no idea I was over here, you'd start to question if it was worth it at all,' a despondent Frelihy admitted, while taking a picture of himself with a skyscraper in the background.

MOTORING

LOCAL learner driver Declan Kerrihan has stated that there's no harm in him driving his car around without a fully licensed driver as a passenger, as he's 'only going up the road' and therefore immune from poor driving decisions and accidents.

Kerrihan, 21, frequently drives his 1.2 L Clio around the roads of his native Lismore on his own, despite the legal requirement of all learner drivers to have a fully licensed driver in their company at all times.

Given the trivial, 'just there and back again' nature of his journeys to and from his friends' homes, to work every day, and into town at the weekend, Kerrihan falls into the category of 'young drivers to whom the learner driver law does not apply', which, coupled with his knowledge of where and when garda checkpoints appear around the Waterford roads,

UNACCOMPANIED LEARNER DRIVER 'JUST GOING UP THE ROAD'

makes him 100 per cent within his rights to drive wherever he wants.

'Learner drivers have, by their very definition, little to no experience of driving, and accident statistics for the year show that they're at risk of causing injury and death when driving by themselves,' said a spokesperson for the Garda Excuses Department.

'But they certainly are very experienced when it comes to excuses and loopholes, which Mr Kerrihan is using to his advantage now. Why, if he's only going "up the road", well, that's grand. There's almost zero chance of him having an accident when he's only going up the road, and as such he doesn't need someone more experienced in the car to tell him when he's going too fast, or what to do when he experiences something

> **'Learner drivers have, by their very definition, little to no experience of driving, and accident statistics for the year show that they're at risk of causing injury and death when driving by themselves'**

he's never encountered before. He's grand. Tip away, young sir.'

Meanwhile, Kerrihan has amended his definition of 'just up the road' to include basically everywhere he drives to, as technically even Donegal is 'just up the road' from Waterford.

WW news

Waterford Whispers News

WORLD NEWS

CRAIC MAY RISE TO 91, FEAR EXPERTS

THE hands of the craic doomsday clock have been moved forward by experts for the first time in nearly 20 years, with experts fearing that the sheer 'gasness' of being Irish may breach the tolerable 'craic = 90' benchmark in the coming weeks.

The combination of St Patrick's Day, the amount of pent-up craic accumulated during Storm Emma, and the dropping of regulations on the sale of alcohol on Good Friday could see the craic in Ireland reach 91, with craicologists at a loss as to what this will do to the fabric of Irish society.

Calls have been made for emergency anti-craic measures to be put in place by the government, in a bid to get the nation to settle the head and catch a hold of themselves

'The craic doomsday clock hasn't been this high since Italia '90'

'before the whole thing is fucked altogether'.

'The craic doomsday clock hasn't been this high since Italia '90,' said Patrick McPaddy, originator of the craic scale during an ill-fated trip to the Isle of Man.

'We need an emergency budget, a USC hike, Irish Water back on the

job. Otherwise we could be heading into a 3-week session that could push this country over the brink into craicmageddon, a craictastrophy, just craicdemonium altogether.'

WWN would advise those looking to avoid the upcoming craicnarok to seek shelter until the summer, when the craic should shift to other countries as all the mad bastards go on holidays.

Suburban Dictionary

'Begrudge-grudger' – an individual who strongly begrudges the fact someone begrudges someone else and their success.

MIDDLE EAST

'YOU GOT OVER US KILLING KIDS ON A BEACH, YOU'LL GET OVER THIS'

IN an effort to better explain the killings of at least 18 Palestinians attending a mass protest at the Gaza–Israel border, Israeli leader Benjamin Netanyahu reminded everyone about how they got over the fact Israeli forces killed some children playing on a beach four years ago.

'Guys, honestly, there's no reason to get so worked up about the slaughter of innocent people. Just look how we all moved on from a targeted airstrike on some kids playing on a Gaza beach. Let's save ourselves some time and energy and just skip to the "getting over it" part,' Netanyahu confirmed.

Although Netanyahu was visibly relieved to be taking a break from accusations of corruption and bribery, he also appeared vexed by the insistence in some quarters that Palestinian lives carry value that is on par with other, non-Palestinian human beings.

'You got over us killing kids on a beach, you'll get over this, I promise you. Nine kids were blown up as they played football and watched the World Cup on a nearby TV back in 2014.

Starting to sound familiar, yeah? This is the first time you've remembered that in a few years, correct? So all I ask is you do the same for this,' Netanyahu added, urging people calling for investigations and inquiries into the latest killings to just relax already.

'Kids, women, the elderly, the innocent, these pesky terms used to humanise our soldiers' target practice are helping no one. We've already investigated the next spate of killings and found ourselves not guilty so you can all move on, thank you.'

AUSTRALIA has been asked to 'quit going on' about how their gun control laws have prevented the senseless loss of innocent lives in their country since being put into place after the 1996 Port Arthur massacre, with USA Second Amendment fans urging the Aussies to stop 'thinking they know everything'.

The chilling massacre of 35 men, women and children in the popular tourist spot of Port Arthur was enough to bring about sweeping new legislation as well as a gun amnesty that saw over 1 million privately

AUSTRALIA THINKS IT'S GREAT BECAUSE IT BANNED GUNS AFTER A MASS SHOOTING

held firearms 'bought back' and destroyed by the Australian government.

With no mass shootings anywhere near the scale of the Port Arthur tragedy in the decades since, Australia is often cited as proof that gun control can help save lives, something that America's favourite gun club, the National Rifle Association, has dismissed as 'coincidence'.

'Yeah, we hear you lads, you're fucking great, give it a rest,' said a spokesperson for the NRA, speaking at the site of the US mass shooting that is bound to have taken place since the beginning of this article.

'You banned guns and there were no more mass shootings, but let me ask you this: what if there was a mass shooting, eh? Where would you be then? Ha, you didn't think of that one, did you?'

The NRA was then asked to explain the similar situation that happened in the UK following the Dunblane massacre, but they ran out of the building with their fingers in their ears.

US-MADE BOMBS NOW CONTAIN CROP SEEDS TO HELP CURB FAMINE IN YEMEN

IN a bid to curb a large-scale famine in Yemen, US defence contractor Lockheed Martin is expanding its munitions factories to meet the rising demand, and has vowed to insert over 200 crop seeds into every single bomb bought by their Saudi customers.

The seeds, ranging from wheat to poppy seeds, are expected to generate hundreds of tonnes of food and heroin over the next several months, with the aim of feeding the millions of starving people affected by the conflict and showing the rest of the world that the United States is trying to help the humanitarian crisis, despite fuelling it with military hardware.

'Bomb survivors will now have an opportunity to grow their own crops between airstrikes,' Frank St John, Lockheed's vice president of tactical missiles, told WWN.

'For every bomb dropped, an acre of land will be fertilised with wheat, barley, or even poppy fields for heroin cultivation,' he added. 'Its a win-win situation for everybody involved in the Yemen war, including the US.'

However, the move has been met with some backlash from the American public, with some complaining about the $2 million cost of the seeds for the American taxpayer.

'To think that $2 million out of our military budget of $824.6 billion will be used to feed non-Americans makes me sick to my stomach,' voiced one Republican. 'That $2 million could have been used to help the 1.56 million homeless people living here.'

Meanwhile, victims of the Yemen famine have welcomed the move, with many affected people now congregating around known bomb targets to avail of the generosity of the US.

'At first I was really angry at the United States for supplying weapons to the Saudis, but now I've changed my mind,' said one Yemeni man we spoke to who was later obliterated by a Lockheed Martin ballistic missile, along with his wife and four children.

300 MILLION AMERICAN GUN OWNERS STOOD BY AND DID NOTHING TO STOP FLORIDA SHOOTING, FINDS REPORT

A RECENTLY published report into the latest school shooting in Florida has found as many as 300 million registered gun owners in America did absolutely nothing to stop a former student fatally shooting 17 people at Marjory Stoneman Douglas High School in Parkland, WWN can confirm.

A week after one of the deadliest mass shootings in modern US history, America's gun owners denied all blame in not acting sooner to stop Nikolas Jacob Cruz, a 19-year-old former student at the school, from executing 14 pupils and three staff members with a military grade assault rifle.

'I was over 3,000 miles away,' one cowardly Californian gun owner defended, despite not doing anything about the previous 188 school shootings in the last 18 years. 'What was I supposed to do? My gun doesn't shoot that far.'

Echoing his wimpy stance, hundreds of millions of Americans also took no responsibility for last week's murders, with many admitting to being confused as to which one they were actually supposed to react to.

'Which 2018 school shooting do you mean?' asked New York resident and self-confessed gun fanatic, Chad Frazer. 'Do you mean the one on 20 January, or the one on the 22nd, or the one on the 23rd, or the one in Philly on the 31st? Or are you talking about February's school shootings, which landed on the 1st, 5th, 9th or the last one on the 14th? Because reacting to them all would be a full-time job for all 300 million of us.'

Meanwhile, US President Donald Trump has since pardoned the rest of America by blaming the entirety of the latest shooting on one man, Deputy Scot Peterson, after he failed to confront the suspect with his semi-automatic handgun.

'Hanging is too good for him,' America's 300 million gun owners later chimed in unison. 'If only we were there, none of this would have ever happened.'

ENVIRONMENT

IDIOT WHALE DIES AFTER EATING 30 KG OF RUBBISH

A WHALE described by marine experts as being a 'complete and utter idiot' was found washed up in Spain with 29 kg of plastic debris in its stomach, WWN can confirm.

The young male sperm whale is believed to have died from 'gastric shock' following an autopsy which found debris, including nets, plastic bags and a jerrycan in the 10-metre-long stomach of the mammal. It is understood inflammation of the inner walls of the abdomen and the whale's poor IQ were the causes of its death.

'We found nearly 30 kg of plastic inside the whale,' expert Carlos Rosario, the director general for the environment in Murcia's government explained. 'What kind of idiot eats that much plastic rubbish and expects to survive?'

Mr Rosario recalled a similar incident last week where a tortoise was caught wearing a plastic beer can holder around its neck like a necklace.

'What kind of idiot eats that much plastic rubbish and expects to survive?'

'I think it's dumber these animals are getting,' he explained, before showing some of the rubbish ingested by the whale. 'Everyone knows plastic bags are dangerous and should never be eaten due to the risks of poisoning or suffocation. Whales are meant to eat plankton and small fish, so it only has itself to blame.'

In 2016, a pod of 13 sperm whales also washed up with plastic rubbish inside them, renewing calls to educate marine life about the dangers of eating synthetic material made from polymers such as polyethylene, PVC and nylon.

'I suppose this is natural selection, and nothing for us smart humans to worry about,' Rosario concluded.

The Solution Zone!

Noting the dire state the world is in today, WWN proposes practical solutions to some of Ireland's and the world's most pressing issues.

Fake News:

– Not sure if the news you're getting is fake or not? Simply check to see if you agree with everything that the source is saying, and has ever said. Then you should be confident that they aren't just telling you what you want to hear.

– If you disagree with the results of a poll, then it's probably fake news. Just ignore it, and allow your opinion to go unchanged.

– When it comes time to vote on a sensitive subject such as a referendum, make sure to get all the facts you need from Facebook, or Twitter, or from a poster that you don't know the source of. They wouldn't be allowed to run it if it wasn't accurate, right?

– When in doubt, always trust the news source that the most people follow. People can't possibly be wrong in such big numbers.

FARMING

500 MILLION RED BULLS SLAUGHTERED ANNUALLY TO MAKE POPULAR ENERGY DRINK

ANIMAL rights activists have called on the world's largest energy drink manufacturers to stop the annual slaughter of 500 million red bulls, urging them to substitute the animals' liquidised genitalia for another ingredient instead.

'It takes 12 pairs of fully grown red bull testicles to make 100 cans of the energy drink,' a spokesperson for PETA explained. 'This is such a waste of life considering the rest of the animal is thrown away, and the impact from breeding so many animals for this purpose is having a huge effect on

> **'It takes 12 pairs of fully grown red bull testicles to make 100 cans of the energy drink'**

carbon emissions and a knock-on effect on the environment.

'Plus, it's just wrong to be drinking sugary blended bovine bollocks like that – it can't be good for consumer health and well-being.'

Established in 1987 in Austria, Red Bull was first founded by entrepreneur Dietrich Mateschitz when he accidentally discovered it after being dared by a friend to drink

liquidised red bull testicles, mixed with children's medicine Calpol 6+ in a soda stream.

'My friend Hans had a pretty fucked up sense of humour. Of course, it sounded awful, but when I tasted that fizzy yellow pissy semen liquid, I knew I was on to something,' Dietrich told a German newspaper in 1992.

Realising the stimulating effects from red bull bollocks, Mateschitz went on to develop the ingredients and packaging to achieve the highest market share of any energy drink in the world, with 6.06 billion cans sold in any one year.

'We have tried black, white, brown and various other colours and types of bull, but the red bull seems to be the best tasting,' a spokesperson for Red Bull later responded. 'We believe it's to do with the red bull urine and semen mix in the liquidation process, and this is what gives consumers their wings.'

Wonderful World of Science

It's impossible to say the word goose if you place your fist inside your mouth. Incidentally, all other words are also impossible to say under these circumstances.

OLD MACDONALD HOMELESS AFTER FARM FORECLOSURE

OLD MacDonald's farm has gone under foreclosure today after he failed to make a series of mortgage repayments on the 400 acre site in the state of Missouri. A court ordered local sheriffs to immediately seize the property, leaving the owner homeless and out on the street.

The 78-year-old farmer said goodbye to his remaining livestock before handing over the keys of his 100-year-old family home to receivers, before then taking some time to address the awaiting world media who were gathered outside.

'I don't know what's going to happen with all these animals,' old MacDonald began, visibly upset at the thought. 'I suppose everyone can safely say now that old MacDonald "had" a farm.'

And on that farm he reportedly had some sheep, cows, pigs, ducks, the majority of whom will now have to be destroyed under Section 47 of the Livestock Act of 1986, which stipulates that foreclosed farm animals would have to be humanely euthanized if they had nowhere else to go.

'With a woof-woof here, a moo-moo there, here a quack, there a quack, everywhere a baa-baa, I'm fucking devastated,' added old MacDonald, before oddly yelling the letters, 'E-I-E-I-O'.

It is understood the 'fully functioning' farm will now be taken back by the banks and later sold on at auction for a fraction of the money old MacDonald had originally owed them.

GINGERS WARNED NOT TO GET ANY BIG IDEAS

THE global ginger community has been officially warned today not to get any big ideas after it was announced that American actor Meghan Markle is to wed ginger and royal, Prince Harry, in spring 2018 at Kensington Palace.

A joint statement released by the British government and Buckingham Palace urged people with red hair to not get their hopes up over the news, pointing out that Prince Harry is a lot wealthier than they are and is of royal blood, so 'don't even go there'.

'This may seem like a turning point in your ginger life,' read the statement. 'But please, refrain from any big moves towards the opposite sex as refusal may cause offence.

'This is a once-off event and you are not likely to see anything like it again in the rest of your miserable life on this planet. Please just carry on doing whatever it is you people do out there, with your Fanta-coloured nether regions.'

The pair became engaged earlier this month, giving hundreds of thousands of red-haired men and women false hope, which was thankfully nipped in the bud by the Palace statement.

'It had to be said,' a royal spokesman explained. 'We've been getting a lot of queries from people afflicted with ginger hair, asking how Harry managed it.

'It would break your heart to see the optimism in their correspondence, but there's no point in leading them on; you just have to be straight up, otherwise they'll all be at it.'

CHRIST IN CRITICAL CONDITION AFTER BIKE ACCIDENT

AVID cyclist Jesus Christ has been rushed to hospital with severe injuries after ploughing his ten-speed racer into the back of a family saloon during rush hour this morning.

Shocked eyewitnesses posed for selfies at the grisly scene, as emergency service workers attended to the wounds of our Lord and Saviour Jesus Christ, following the sickening collision at 8.45 a.m.

Although many expressed concern for the well-being of the Lamb of God, many criticised his actions prior to the crash, claiming that JC was not concentrating on the road when the smash occurred.

'I yelled, "Hi, Christ on a bike, watch yourself!"'

said one onlooker, who bore first-hand witness to our Lord's hardship on the crossroads.

'He was going way too fast, weaving in and out through traffic, fuckin' texting, so he was… and then smash. All these deities on bicycles are a menace in the city. You can't keep up with them. Just the other week a bus nearly mounted the footpath trying to avoid Buddha on a BMX.'

Emergency service workers have yet to ascertain the extent of Jesus's injuries, following initial confusion about pre-existing holes in his hands and his sides and a complete lack of a pulse.

'I LOVED HIS MUSIC' – TRUMP PAYS TRIBUTE TO MARTIN LUTHER KING

PRESIDENT Donald Trump has led the tributes to mark the 50th anniversary of the assassination of civil rights leader Dr Martin Luther King Jr.

King, whose public orations and leadership during the fight for civil rights in America in the 1960s marked him out as one of the most commanding, progressive and influential figures in the history of the United States of America, was commended by Trump, who remarked, 'On this day we never forget how cool his music was. Loved that guy.'

Trump went on to list off a number of hit songs by a variety of black artists who came to prominence in the 60s, leading many to speculate the normally on-top-of-things president had mistaken King for someone else. Confirmation of this error

by the president later came in the form of another tweet in which he spoke fondly of working with King on the set of one episode of *The Fresh Prince of Bel Air* he had a cameo on in the 90s.

King's non-violent protests earned him a Nobel Prize for Peace in 1964, with many of his impassioned speeches advocating for the equal rights of African Americans, as well as imploring industries to protect, maintain and enhance the rights of workers.

'To think he played piano despite being blind, he truly was an above-average American who one could argue is as great as me in many ways, not all ways, but many,' Trump concluded in an emotional address in front of the press, confounding those who decry his lack of gravitas or wisdom.

RELIGION

SCIENTOLOGY TO TEAM UP WITH CATHOLIC CHURCH FOR SOME MAD SHIT ALTOGETHER

TWO of the biggest religious organisations on the planet are to put aside their decades-old differences and come together for an unforgettable team-up that experts are expecting to be 'batshit bananas altogether'.

After accepting that they share more common ground than differences, the Catholic Church and the Church of Scientology will merge to form the Church of Catholic Scientology, seamlessly weaving the two belief systems into one wild and crazy story about how Jesus came to earth on a stray asteroid before giving up his life on the cross at the hands of the evil intergalactic warlord Kornok.

The two churches will still keep their long-held traditions of odd ceremonies, for-profit business models and oppression of women and homosexuals, but will seek to add 'loads more new shit' to drum up

> ## 'You like Catholicism? You like mad sci-fi shit? Then you're going to love CCS!'

new subscribers, sorry, followers, to help them survive through what is being described as 'a tricky fiscal period'.

'You like Catholicism? You like mad sci-fi shit? Then you're going to love CCS!' read a statement from the newly combined churches, whose Hollywood members include Tom Cruise and Mel Gibson, together at last.

'Instead of the body of Christ, you're going to get the body of Xenu. Instead of audits, you're going to get

confession boxes with robot priests. Instead of keeping women silent and frowning on medical science, you're going to get… well, no, that'll stay actually. And the collection plate going around, that stays too. It's going to be out of this world! Literally!'

The new merger has been derided by atheists who insist that nobody could possibly believe in such a ludicrous exploitation of people's need to believe in something more than themselves, but so far the CCS has had no trouble whatsoever getting people to sign up.

Parish Notes

Gluten-free communion now available, but if you think God wants your poor genetics in heaven then you've another thing coming.

NEW FIGURES SHOW STEADY INCREASE IN FUCKING IDIOTS

DESPITE hopes that the rise of readily available information on just about every conceivable topic via the internet would help to curb the number of fucking idiots in the world, troubling new data has shown that the figure continues to rise year on year.

With high-speed wireless broadband granting access to a databank of the world's knowledge directly through our mobile phones and computers, fucking idiots were considered a 'dying breed' by many who surmised that there was no way we as a species could have so much information at our fingertips and yet still be so uninformed and ignorant.

However, it appears that this hope was ill-founded, as the internet has caused even more people, some of whom started out quite rational and well-informed, to rapidly lose not just their minds, but their fucking minds altogether.

'It seems that the ability to fact-check yourself before making an easily refuted and totally inaccurate statement does not prevent a fucking idiot from doing just that,' sighed Dr Murahasa McGuinness, senior researcher for the World Idiot Monitoring Organisation.

'You would think that today, arguments on social media would last as long as it took to just do a quick Google search and get the full details of whatever you're talking about, but it seems idiots are happy to circumvent all that and go straight to anger while doubling down on their idiotic points of view. But more seriously, it seems other people aren't checking the idiots turning into idiots themselves… they're multiplying. This is an epidemic.'

If you disagree with anything in this fact-based article, it's very possible that you may have succumbed to being a fucking idiot. Please seek education immediately.

MIDDLE EAST

STORMY DANIELS KILLED IN SYRIAN AIRSTRIKE

ADULT film star Stormy Daniels has reportedly been killed last night in a US led airstrike in Syria, WWN can confirm.

The controversial porn actress had apparently travelled to the Middle Eastern country on Thursday in what friends and family members are saying was an unusual move by the dead 39-year-old.

'We have no idea how she got there,' a close friend said last night. 'It's just not a country Stormy would ever visit on a whim, so we're all very upset and confused as to why she would go to such a dangerous place, considering the predicted missile strikes.'

Investigators on the ground believe Ms Daniels was apparently filming a documentary when over 50 tomahawk missiles accidentally hit the location she was at, obliterating her and a number of other American women who just happened to be there at the time.

'Coincidentally, several other women who have accused the US President of sexual misconduct in the past have also been killed in the airstrike,' a US military commander confirmed. 'What they were doing there, we don't know, but it seems they are all dead now and that's all we can say on the matter.'

President Trump ordered a strike on Syria on Friday in response to last

weekend's alleged chemical weapons attack, despite having no evidence.

THE religious community has been shocked by the news that Mary, mother to Jesus Christ, is to take God to court over unpaid child maintenance payments dating back thousands of years.

Described as an 'absentee father' in court documents seen by WWN, the deity could be in line to pay child support costs running into the millions when interest is added.

VIRGIN MARY TO SUE GOD OVER UNPAID CHILD SUPPORT

'Technically God has billions of children, so I think this legal action opens our client up to financial ruin

if the courts rule in the favour of someone we can only describe as a disgruntled and scorned woman,' a solicitor acting on behalf of God told reporters outside a court earlier today.

While God would only be liable to pay for 18 years of child support, it appears He is reluctant to do so.

'My client's work means he isn't even on the planet and he's expected to abide by the ruling of a court here on Earth? And where is Joseph's part in all this?' the solicitor added amidst a flurry of questions from the press pack.

Legal scholars have speculated that Mary's case will centre around whether or not she registered God as the father of the child at the time of the birth.

'She's only after a free house off the council,' explained one Catholic man on a right-wing forum, who admitted to being conflicted and confused by the case.

AMERICA

GUNS TO PHASE OUT AMERICANS BY 2050

A DISTURBING report issued by the International Centre For Research (ICFR) has estimated that guns are on course to phase out Americans by 2050, WWN has learned.

With the number of people suffering horrific and violent gun deaths in America exceeding 33,000 per year, it is believed when this harrowing statistic is combined with an unwavering commitment from politicians to do nothing, the result will be the total eradication of all 320 million Americans by 2050.

'If current trends continue, the last two standing will go down in a blaze of depressing glory sometime in late 2050,' explained head of the report Duncan Morrow.

The ICFR report makes for truly upsetting reading, and begs for immediate action to be taken in relation to a number of competing problems which can all be identified as contributing to America's gun deaths problem. However, leading Republican politicians who have received the report could only confirm how quickly it burned when placed on an open fire.

'I'm here to reassure you, you may be scared after what happened recently, but America will always be a place that is safe for you,' President Donald Trump said in a press conference in which he talked directly to an assortment of worried firearms, in a bid to reassure all guns that no harm would come to them in these troubling times.

Those desperately crying out for action in the wake of tragic death after tragic death after tragic death after tragic death have been incorrectly told it is normal that someone can legally buy an AR-15 rifle before they can purchase beer, and not to worry as other non-gun things kill more Americans every year and something should be done about that instead.

Others suffering insurmountable grief and pain after learning of yet more carnage facilitated by politicians paid by the NRA not to change laws have been told to reconvene in the usual places in public and online to voice their anger next time something like this happens.

Summer on the 39

Memoirs of an undercover Spanish student

Chapter Three:

Now that I am securely embedded within the Spanish student community, it is time for my espionage to really begin. I must learn as much as I can from the Irish public transport system before I go back to Spain in 10 months. So far, I have been travelling mostly by bus, and I have found some interesting differences between Dublin and Spain. There is a much greater sense of camaraderie on the buses here. Irish people are almost always courteous to their bus driver, never leaving without thanking him. None of my 43 fellow Spanish students thank the bus driver as we get on or off – perhaps that is why I notice a sense of hostility towards us from the Irish people on the bus as our journey begins? Other than that, the journey is very pleasant on a Dublin bus, although I am pretty sure there was a man under the influence of heroin shouting loudly into a Nokia 6610 about how he was going to slash someone's face, and another man making what we believed to be racist remarks towards a lady in a burka, although the lad assured everyone that he was 'only messing'. Like I say, camaraderie!

NORTH KOREA

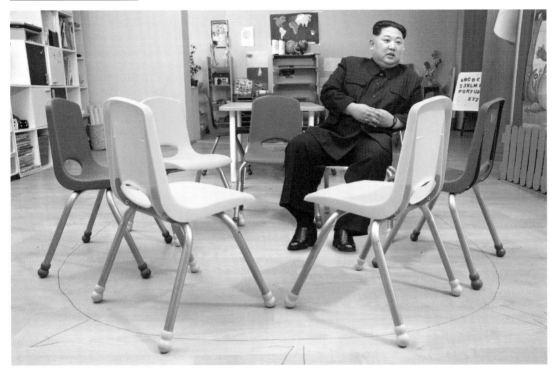

NORTH Korean insiders have revealed for the first time the true effect US President Donald Trump's comments about Kim Jong-un's weight have had on the rotund dictator, WWN can report.

'He's barely eating his daily tub of ice cream. He just picks at it once he's finished the first two litres of it,' explained one official speaking under the condition of anonymity.

Jong-un surprised his most trusted allies when he confided in them that he felt he should join a Weight Watchers class, however his mind was changed when several hundred staff were called to his official residence to reassure him he was the greatest beauty the world had ever seen.

It is believed Jong-un was taken aback by the personal nature of the remarks from Trump, with the North Korean leader presuming personal

KIM JONG-UN ATTENDS FIRST MEETING OF PYONGYANG WEIGHT WATCHERS

'We thought he'd gotten over being called fat, but today he just organised this Weight Watchers meeting himself'

attacks would be off the table as both he and Donald Trump edged closer to organising the nuclear annihilation of one another's peoples.

'It's one thing to say you want to kill everyone and destroy a country, but fat shaming, c'mon, that's a low blow,' added a source.

'We thought he'd gotten over being called fat, but today he just organised this Weight Watchers meeting himself,' shared one source as he looked into a room of empty chairs surrounding the leader.

'He's just sitting there with tears streaming down his face. We don't

have the heart to tell him that the reason he's the only one in the meeting is that everyone else is dying of starvation. He has literally eaten the country's entire supply of cheese. I am not saying this for comic effect. We have so little food that those 47 Cheesestrings he ate for breakfast were all we had left. Please someone help us,' added the source.

Jong-un asked for privacy as he stepped on the weighing scales at the meeting. However, loud squeals of delight could be heard coming from inside the room.

'We fixed the scales so they would max out at nine-and-a-half stone. Last time he weighed himself, he executed the guy who made the scales after it incorrectly broke under his weight,' concluded the source as he prepared to tell his leader how slim he looked during last night's burger eating contest.

PROPERTY

ELON MUSK PURCHASES HOLLOWED-OUT VOLCANO FOR NO PARTICULAR REASON

BILLIONAIRE tech guru Elon Musk has dropped $1.1 billion on his new home: a specially designed, geothermally heated cave in the base of a hollowed-out volcano somewhere in the Pacific Ocean, which Musk states he will use for 'chilling out, nothing evil'.

SpaceX and Tesla CEO Musk has made huge strides in recent years in the fields of private space exploration, off-planet colonisations, flamethrower design and sinister grins, with the 47-year-old becoming the first person to successfully launch a commercial road vehicle into space for no particular reason.

> **'It's just my home away from home, in case I need to get away from it all for a nuclear winter or two'**

His new volcanic home is said to include a hyperloop station where he will be able to take his own high-speed pneumatic bullet train to wherever he wants in the world, as well as a launch pad for SpaceX's bespoke Falcon Heavy rockets, with Musk referring to the property as 'a bit of a fixer-upper' at the minute.

'Lair? No, this is just my gaff,' laughed Musk, for longer than we were comfortable with.

'It's just my home away from home, in case I need to get away from it all for a nuclear winter or two. It's got nothing that any other property hasn't got: ensuite bathroom, kitchen, sleeping quarters for 1,000 henchmen, secret research lab, secret testing facility, secret bunker, secret Nespresso machine in the bedroom. It's just somewhere I can relax and continue my masterplan. Wait, did I say masterplan? I meant plan. Just a normal plan.'

Musk is said to be happy in his new home, but has admitted that the place could do with a white cat or two.

The Solution Zone!

Noting the dire state the world is in today, WWN proposes practical solutions to some of Ireland's and the world's most pressing issues.

YouTube Stars:

– You are never more than 50 feet away from a YouTube megastar that you didn't know even existed. Always be prepared to be trampled by an onrush of their fans as they attempt to meet their hero.

– You are not safe from YouTube stars, even after death. It's very possible that your corpse may be used as material for a vlog, and there's nothing you can do about it. Always look your best, is what we're saying.

– In ten years' time, these people will be your boss. It is best to accept this now, and attempt to get in their favour. It'll only make life easier in the long run.

– Thanks to the money YouTube stars can make, there has never been a better time to have a kid, and immediately put them to work by recording them playing video games, doing make up tutorials, etc.

– Four out of every ten middle-aged men start a YouTube vlog video series as part of their midlife crisis. Do not become one of these men.

– Some people are still mistakenly wasting their time invested in reading about politics and news in general. They do this despite the fact there are over 433,456 separate videos of 'Irish people try X, Y and Z for the first time'.

– 'YouTube star' is a legally protected term like 'doctor' or 'dietician' so remember you can only refer to yourself as a YouTube star if one of your videos has reached 40 views.

– Many people believe if you simply stop watching a YouTube star's videos they will go away. This is incorrect, as they are also on Instagram trying to sell you FitTea.

– If you followed a YouTube star's 5-minute make-up tutorial video but it took you over 45 minutes to complete, you can sue the YouTuber for emotional distress.

– Remember, be kind to YouTube stars; you never know what they're going through. Many of them suffer from a rare condition known as higuysneurothermia, which leaves them unable to start a video with any phrase other than 'Hi guys'.

WW news

Waterford Whispers News

ENTERTAINMENT

TELEVISION

FAIR CITY TO BE OUTSOURCED TO INDIA

IRELAND'S national broadcaster RTÉ has announced some major changes to the popular soap opera *Fair City* today, following news that the production was to be relocated as part of its decision to sell 8.64 acres of land for €107.5 million to Cairn Homes.

A total of 220 people who currently work on the programme were offered a significant redundancy by RTÉ chiefs, who then later confirmed that the entire set will be relocated to Mumbai in India, while a cast of new actors will also be outsourced to the south Asian country.

'We can't wait to step foot in Kareshtown,' said actor Rajesh Numar, who will now be playing the part of Robbie in the new series. 'Never before have I read such a wondrous script. The cult storyline is really good, but my only hope now is that my fellow countrymen can write such amazing things. Groundbreaking stuff.' It is expected that the new writing team will focus more on Indian-based topics, some of which the new producers say were a bit too close to the bone for commissioners at the Dublin-based TV station.

'We won't be going down the gang rape route as one of the RTÉ lawyers had a stroke when we pitched that idea,' explained producer Ramesh Patel, 'but do expect some Bollywood-style song and dance in McKrishna's pub. I honestly can't wait to get started on this.' Fans of the show have welcomed the move.

'They can't be bleedin' worse than the shower that were in it,' said one fan on Twitter. 'I only look at the thing to take the piss out of it.'

The new series of *Fair City* is to air in April this year.

Suburban Dictionary

'Life sentence' – a short stint of around five to eight years, usually handed out for the most extreme crimes in Ireland.

Summer on the 39

Memoirs of an undercover Spanish student

Chapter Four:

Today I decided to travel by the Dublin tram system called the Luas, which is not pronounced anything like what you may think it to be – another example of Irish humour? I opted to use the Luas as I felt the Dublin bus commuters were growing tired of not being able to get on the bus during rush-hour traffic due to a huge number of Spanish students who were only travelling to the next bus stop, which was literally within sight. The Luas is a fine piece of transport, although I'm not sure my handlers back in Spain will know what to make of the decision to run a tramline through a city centre area that is also shared by pedestrians, bicycles, buses, taxis, rickshaw operators, private cars, and what appears to be an amphibious jeep/Viking boat, all at peak-hour traffic. During my journey across the city, we nearly hit nine cyclists – a record, my fellow passenger assured me, before jumping off at the next stop because he saw someone checking for tickets.

Fair City

THE HAGUE

RONAN KEATING 'FAIRYTALE OF NEW YORK' TRIAL BEGINS AT THE HAGUE

FORMER Boyzone General Ronan Keating was in a defiant mood this morning as he arrived at The Hague to face charges of crimes against humanity surrounding his year 2000 butchering of The Pogues' classic Christmas hit, 'Fairytale of New York'.

The vicious assault launched on the ears of festive music fans was short-lived, but the damage done that year can still be felt almost 18 years later, with Spotify playlists and Apple Music searches sometimes throwing up the Keating version instead of the original.

Keating, speaking through an interpreter who speaks fluent shhhh, remained emotionless in the dock as the charges were read against him, confident that if they didn't nail him for 'When You Say Nothing At All', they'd never convict him for this.

'We will find today, with the evidence available to us, that Mr Keating did purposefully and deliberately record and distribute a horrendous version of "Fairytale of New York" onto an unsuspecting public,' read the statement from the prosecution.

'This was a senseless, cruel attack on people, at Christmastime no less. There are children who heard the Ronan Keating version before any other, and are still dealing with their feelings about it today. Mr Keating, you have shown no remorse for your actions up to this point, and it is the duty of this court to ensure that humanity finally receives the justice it deserves.' Meanwhile, original 'Fairytale' singer Shane MacGowan has testified that the Keating version is what turned him to a life of alcoholism, having never touched a drop before he heard it.

HUNGOVER MAN SPENDS DAY WATCHING WEIRD SHIT ON YOUTUBE

A COUNTY Waterford man is expected to remain on the couch for the majority of the day watching weird YouTube videos while nursing a considerable hangover, WWN has learned.

Colm O'Brien, who went out for the one last night, but ended home at 4 a.m., peeled himself off the bed at 2 p.m. today in a bid to source some water, Panadol, anything to get him through his thumping headache and inability to think of anything but the pain.

After several agonising minutes searching for the plug part of his charger, O'Brien slithered into his dark sitting room, curtains closed in a bid to hide from any unsuspecting callers or sales people, leaving them ajar enough for his pizza order later.

'Why don't takeaways open before 5 p.m.?' he muttered to himself, closing his Just Eat app in disgust. 'Suppose I better throw on some shite on YouTube to pass the time.' Carefully scrolling through DanTDM recommendations and epic fails compilations – previously searched for by his young children – O'Brien's channel listings for UFOs, ancient civilisations and David Icke finally popped up.

'Ah, yes! Elongated alien skulls from Peru!' he exclaimed, now pulling the lever to recline his chair. 'I might throw on some Illuminati stuff after this, see what the new world order are up to these days.' However, the attention of the son of two was then diverted to a recommended video about some 19-year-old talking about his first DMT trip.

'I'd give that stuff a right lash, so I would,' he said, before suddenly getting that electric shock stroke thing in his head that he always gets when he's hungover. 'Ah fuck this, I'm never drinking again.'

EXCLUSIVE

NEW TEMPLATE 'APOLOGY' ISSUED FOR MEN ACCUSED OF SEXUAL HARASSMENT

AS A DIRECT result of the increasing number of famous and prominent men issuing statements of apology for harassing and assaulting people, there has been a push to provide them with a template stock apology/PR statement so as to avoid further enraging and insulting their victims.

Written and drawn up by a vast array of experts in not sounding like narcissistic and egotistical abusers of power and trust, it is hoped that whoever is next alleged to have carried out heinous and stomach-turning acts can have a ready-made apology, which is incapable of doing any further damage, and providing, at the very least, a genuine acknowledgement of the damage and hurt they have caused.

'This template has been chosen with the aim of stopping someone from creating a statement which is essentially, "Shit, I'm so sorry I was caught, but at the same time, I don't remember doing any of these things,"' explained someone with a functioning brain, alluding to several statements

'Who knows? The next person who admits to sexual assault might actually present themselves to the nearest police station

previously made by celebrities in which they admit that the allegations are true without actually admitting it.

In place of vague sentences, which stop short of admitting any direct responsibility for anything ranging from lewd comments and groping to the attempted rape of a child, come simple and brief passages that communicate the acceptance of full responsibility and make no mention of empty talk of 'seeking help' or having been 'going through something'.

'We didn't think it was a novel idea at first, but then every apology that was issued just seemed a step closer to a more articulate form of not owning the fuck up to illegal and abusive acts,' added another person

with a healthy reserve of empathy and common sense.

The template replaces such trivial phrases as 'I'm now aware this was not appropriate behaviour' with 'I knew all along sexually harassing people was wrong, but I didn't care and I only care now that my career and reputation has been significantly damaged', leading to the real possibility that people reading such statements in the future will not scream with rage when they get to the end of the final paragraph.

'Who knows? The next person who admits to sexual assault might actually present themselves to the nearest police station instead of hiring an expensive law firm and a boat-load of PR experts,' confirmed a third person in possession of the most basic understanding of being a decent person.

Elsewhere, women have been forced to reaffirm the fact that no medals will be issued to men who take to social media to confirm they have never sexually harassed or abused women.

MOVIE NEWS

WOMAN HAS SEX WITH FISH MAN WINS BEST PICTURE AT OSCARS

THE enchanting tale, directed by Guillermo del Toro, won several awards last night as Oscar voters connected to a story of how a woman totally has sex with a fish man.

Filled to the gills with allusions to cross-species fish-fucking, *Woman Has Sex with Fish Man* beat out other contenders for Best Picture such as *Get Out, Call Me by Your Name* and *Lady Bird*, which dealt with different but equally worthy themes.

'It's the best film I've seen about a fish man totally going to town on a woman with his weird fish genitalia this year. I can say that with some certainty,' confirmed one Oscar Academy voter, thrilled to see the film triumph at the film industry's biggest night of the year, while Meryl Streep was overheard at an Oscar after-party remarking 'Fish-fucking films are my jam'.

In a night of firsts, which also saw Jordan Peele become the first black person to win Best Original Screenplay, *Woman Has Sex with Fish Man* became the first movie centred around going to funky town with a fish man to be nominated for 13 Oscars.

'This award is for those who doubted me when I said people would pay money to see a movie about a lady boinking a fish, thank you,' director Guillermo del Toro said in his acceptance speech for Best Director, bringing the total awards *Woman Has Sex with Fish Man* won on the night to four.

Industry experts have not ruled out a flurry of new films being greenlit by Hollywood studios which deal with amorous amphibian–human humping after the awards success of *Woman Has Sex with Fish Man*.

Elsewhere, equality campaigners descended on social media to criticise the award for Best Actress being awarded to a woman for the 90th year in a row.

CELEBS TO JUST STOP GOING TO THE BEACH

SINGERS, actors, models and reality TV personalities have angrily stated that until the press stops snapping pictures of them in their bikinis and swimming trunks, they're just going to stay at home, watching TV, fully dressed.

Fat celebs, skinny celebs, and celebs who climb on rocks have 'wised up' to the decades-old media trend of shoring up slow news days with tawdry, long-lens shots of scantily clad famous people as they lounge on beaches and hotel pools around the world.

With even the lowliest, z-level reality no-mark unable to go anywhere near a body of water without ending up as part of a 'too fat/ too skinny' article, celebrities have united for the first time in a bid to stamp out the process, or at least get a cut of the action.

'Look at this: "Ben Affleck goes shirtless at the beach". Now tell me who the fuck wants to see that?' read an open letter from the International Union of Famous People.

'We appreciate that there's a tranche of younger, media-hungry celebs who court the press by hitting the sands, but what about poor Jennifer Lawrence, who just wants to take her metal detecting equipment and go looking for old bottle caps on a nice day? Until you newspaper bastards learn how to have a bit of manners and respect, it's a 100 per cent beach boycott from us. Let's see how you fill page six now, dickheads. 'With the boycott already in full effect, fans of celebrity gossip have admitted that they're finding it hard to get through the day without knowing whether or not Helen Mirren 'still has it'.

REFERENDUM CALLED ON WHETHER NATION DEFINITIVELY LIKES OR DISLIKES SAOIRSE RONAN

'IT HAS never been more important to ask of the nation that most challenging question: in light of her third Oscar nomination, do we like or dislike Saoirse Ronan? There needs to be a definitive answer.' A rare foray into overt political discourse from President Michael D. Higgins has set in motion a snap referendum on the esteem in which the Irish public holds Saoirse Ronan.

Depending on who you ask, the Carlow native is a preeminent acting talent in Hollywood who has no peers; to others she isn't even from Carlow at all. With such divisive views held by many, a referendum was inevitable.

'While it is unconventional, I have taken the president's words into account and the Saoirse Ronan Referendum will take place next week. However, I have not yet decided how I will vote. This is a matter of conscience, and I will not cast my vote lightly,' Taoiseach Leo Varadkar declared today via a carefully focus-grouped press release.

If the nation votes 'dislike' it will require a drastic change to the nation's constitution whereby the Irish public can no longer simply begin loving a public figure after America takes notice of them and praises the individual.

'It's madness, they haven't considered the legislative implications, and what's more, Saoirse was transcendent in *Lady Bird*. An acting triumph,' one pro-Saoirse supporter, who hasn't seen the film for which the actress is nominated, shared.

To many pro-Saoirse advocates, that a referendum is needed at all is baffling in the extreme. However, there remains an alleged 'silent majority' who just don't seem to like the successful actress.

'I can't tell you why someone's existence irritates me so, but it does. And no, she isn't just some outlet towards which I can hurl all my unhappiness. Don't even try to open that wound,' confirmed one anti-Saoirse voter, who labelled the actress 'Who? Never heard of her' in the comments section of TheJournal.ie.

THE line-up to this year's Longitude festival has been celebrated in an ecstatic fashion by lovers of contemporary rap and hip-hop music. However, the Marlay Park festival is said to also be doubling up as the most effective way to discover whether or not you are still cool, experts in coolness can confirm.

Failure to recognise even one artist on the impressive bill is now the most expedient way to make peace with the fact you are not cool, but it has been known to elicit an obscene amount of moaning too.

'I don't know any of the acts; they sound shite to me. I demand you change the line-up immediately,' one former cool person, Dermot Kilrudd, said as he shouted at the sky, unable to accept that he's about as cool as an ice cube in a volcano.

Kilrudd, like so many music fans, once had a keen interest in cool music, but last paid attention to what was cool when Franz Ferdinand and The Strokes were in their heyday and now prefers to just give out about things he doesn't understand or 'get'.

'This is bullshit. I want it to be full of cool music I like or else it should be cancelled,' added Kilrudd, who hasn't been to a gig in about three years.

Previously, it was only possible to ascertain if people

NOT KNOWING ANY ACT ON LONGITUDE LINE-UP A SIGN YOU'RE NO LONGER COOL

were no longer cool if they only ever expressed a like for movies, songs or TV shows pre-2005, wore

crocs, or recently shared memes you had first seen over a year ago.

Those individuals, who have been careful to point out they do know the likes of Joey Bada$$, Migos, Sampha and Solange but just think they're shite, have been told to 'let it go'.

Elsewhere, your great-grandfather remembers when Longitude was a decent festival.

MUSIC

HAVE NO DISCERNIBLE PERSONALITY? HERE ARE 4 TAYLOR SWIFT SONGS YOU'LL LOVE

ARE you one of the poor unfortunates who, try as you might, can't seem to exert enough effort to make a mark in conversations and interactions with friends, family and co-workers? When it comes down to it, is it just too exhausting to force yourself to like cool-people things?

Do your interests, hobbies and pastimes fail to mark you out as decipherable from any of the other seven billion odd people on the planet? Have people called you Joanne, Leanne, Karen, Rachel, Rebecca or Jane when that's clearly not your name and, hang on, you've known the person incorrectly calling you Jane for three years? Do they... do they not know your name?

Are you human kitchen roll? Always needed but often forgotten in the weekly shop?

Brilliant! Then this bland list of bland songs by bland Taylor Swift is the kind of bland music that'll get you shaking your hips in that forgettable way you do that no one can recall because you're not really standing out with your bold opinions on... do you have any strongly held opinions? We can't remember. Sorry, that's on us. We should have paid closer attention to you, Jane.

1) Blank Space
That thundering chorus that comes in like a yawn abandoned half way through being completed. Alright, hell yeah! Gentle, inconsequential music for the win!

2) Call It What You Want
Oof! Listen to those drums, borrowed from songs that actually raise your heart rate except here they've been dulled down so as not to risk such a thing from happening.

3) I Did Something Bad
Featuring the word 'shit' – we're into unchartered territory. We had no idea you were such a badass.

4) End Game
With a 'feat.' from Ed Sheeran. Hold up, we can't take how game changing this game changer is. Tay Swfitie Biftie Nifty paired with the greatest guitarist of all time?

Parish Notes

American tourists expected in town there in the next few minutes, if you could all 'culchie it up', please. Thank you.

RADIO

LOCAL COMMUNITY RADIO HOST KNOWS NO ONE IS LISTENING

THE host of an unpopular local radio show has been broadcasting across the airwaves with his usual zany and bubbly enthusiasm despite knowing, deep down, there isn't a soul out there listening to him.

Barry Hartigan, host of the Sunday morning slot between 2 and 4 a.m. on Waterford's second most popular radio station catering to the Dungarvan area of the county, Waterford Waves FM, is attempting to provide the listening public with a rip-roaring journey through the biggest hits of the 80s, interspersed with idle chit-chat, even though he's almost 100 per cent certain no one has tuned in to his show.

'And that was Duran Duran with "Rio". We're back on *Hartigan Harps On*, on Waterford Waves FM, your home of the hits,' Hartigan said with a cheery tone that hid from the non-existent listener the very real presence of melancholy within Hartigan's soul.

'You guys out there probably want another monster '80s hit, and I'm not going to disappoint: here's Sting and the Police,' Hartigan added, before slumping in his chair and staring off into nothingness for the duration of 'Roxanne'.

Hartigan then abandoned plans for the usual 'What's That Sound?' slot that appeals to listeners to ring or text in with their guesses about the source of a mystery sound after the last 12 weeks resulted in zero listeners responding.

Knowing he no longer had the energy reserves to fake being happy about broadcasting at 3.34 a.m. to no one, Hartigan lined up the full 5 minutes and 55 seconds of 'Bohemian Rhapsody' despite the Queen hit being released in 1975, a decision a younger, less weary Hartigan would never have made.

'You guys out there probably want another monster '80s hit, and I'm not going to disappoint: here's Sting and the Police'

MAN STILL DEFENDING *GODFATHER PART III*

THE much maligned and criticised final chapter in the *Godfather* movie trilogy is still being defended by one local man, despite the majority of people conceding to the reality that it is an awful pile of drivel.

With the misfortune of having to meet the expectations set by the previous two instalments, regarded by many to be among the greatest movies ever made, *The Godfather: Part III* became a huge disappointment to even the most die-hard film fans upon its release in 1990.

Despite this, some 28 years later, Tramore resident Stephen Boyle still insists on defending the film, often without being prompted by anyone to do so.

'It's not that bad like. It's actually pretty good,' Boyle explained to WWN even though it really isn't anything of the sort.

'But like Andy Garcia is pretty good in it,' Boyle added, despite the fact that Andy Garcia isn't very good in it. Andy Garcia is sort of very bad in it.

'The plot isn't as bad as everyone says and the acting is obviously top notch,' Boyle continued, flailing about in a sea of misguided opinions, before drowning.

No one close to Boyle can shed any light on why the 33-year-old is so insistent in his defence of the steaming pile of shite that many refer to as 'the third Godfather movie'.

'Well, first off, it's weird because as far as I'm concerned, there's only ever been two Godfather movies,' explained close Boyle associate Colm Murrin. 'It's usually around 1 a.m. at parties or at the dessert portion of dinner in a restaurant he brings it up. Ruins the night for everyone, the deluded fool.'

RTÉ LAUNCHES INTERNAL INQUIRY AFTER IT ACCIDENTALLY MAKES GOOD SHOW

CONFUSED senior commissioning staff at the national broadcaster, RTÉ, have launched an internal inquiry after learning one of its shows is being well received by the public.

'We've no idea how this happened; we're very sorry. We at RTÉ endeavour to serve the public, and we realise we have failed in this case. We promise to get it right next time,' the RTÉ PR department confirmed, mistakenly using an old template press release they use after every new programme airs.

The inquiry will require some staff to closely examine the broadcaster's commissioning process to find out how a good show was accidentally made.

'We can assure you, this was never our intention. But in the meantime, while we try to get to the bottom of the error, we've ordered 19 spin-off shows related to it, and the stars of the show will appear on *Cutting Edge*, *The Late Late Show*, *The Ray D'Arcy Show*, *Breakfast Republic*, whatever Eoghan McDermott is presenting these days and *The Today Show* for the next 6 weeks,' RTÉ confirmed.

In a bid to capitalise on the unintended success of a show connecting with a non-rural audience under 99 years of age, RTÉ has confirmed they will repeat the show on RTÉ 2 at 2.15 a.m. on Mondays, and will put 14 minutes of ads on the RTÉ Player version.

MOVIE NEWS

WORLD GOOD FOR SUPERHERO MOVIES NOW, CHEERS

THE global cinema-going community has come together to pen an open letter to movie studios, staunchly asserting that when it comes to movies about superheroes, we're good, thanks.

Although many people consider the release of *Iron Man* to be the birth of the current superhero craze, the trend began back in the early 2000s, with the success of the first of 18 *Spider-Man* movies sending studios dashing to create as many franchises ending in '-man' as they could, as quickly as they could.

After nearly 20 years of watching CGI characters bounce off against each other while being bombarded with the sounds of breaking glass and crumbling masonry, audiences have united in their desire to watch just one movie where someone doesn't inherit incredible powers before using them to battle someone with practically identical, slightly more sinister powers for two-and-a-half hours.

'It's not you, it's us,' read the letter to the heads of Disney, Sony, Fox and Bord Scannán na hÉireann.

'Yes, we will admit that we've gone to pretty much every one of these things for the past 20 years, so thanks for that… but honestly, what else have you got, eh? We've given you all a serious break when it comes to new ideas, so surely in that time you've cooked up something in the background, right? A passion project or two? Something that isn't super-team-mash-up-city-destruction part 9? Let's have a bit of that, please.'

Studios have responded by cancelling their upcoming superhero schedule for the next four years, meaning anyone who really wanted a Bananaman movie is shit out of luck.

DIE HARD SEQUEL WILL SEE BRUCE WILLIS DIE OF OLD AGE

THE much anticipated and inevitable sequel in the *Die Hard* franchise will see the iconic character of John McClane, played by Bruce Willis, finally meet his end after being bested by a villainous foe named old age.

McClane, well versed in fighting off terrorists with German accents, will prove no match for the slow march of time with the retired NYPD officer succumbing to complications arising from pneumonia.

Always with a quip at the ready, McClane's body, ravaged by time, will take to the screen for an adrenaline-rush ride which sees it attempt to fend off the mortality we are all subjected to.

'John is the hero we all aspire to be: brave, cool and resourceful. But yeah, he's going to get done in by old age, with room for the usual explosions,' Willis enthused in an interview with the *Hollywood Reporter*.

While McClane breathes in some final breaths, there will be time for some of the *Die Hard* franchise's trademark action scenes.

'A helicopter crashes into the side of the hospital; ISIS spread a nerve agent through the air-conditioning system, but McClane? McClane will actually be just slowly slipping away surrounded by friends and family in the ICU on the 12th floor. It's very moving, while the action elsewhere is very violent,' Willis explained of giving the beloved character the right send off.

PLAYSTATION 4 CHRISTMAS PRESENT FINALLY UPDATED

A COUNTY Waterford teenager whose family home is dependent on rural broadband is to finally begin using his PlayStation 4 Christmas present today after it finished updating itself, WWN has learned.

Jason Mackey, 14, had reportedly been waiting for five days for his console to catch up with its latest software update, before then realising the actual games had to update too.

'I fired it up at 9 a.m. Christmas Day morning,' the boy's father, Dave Mackey, explained. 'Then this blue screen came on insisting that we had to update the PlayStation, which took the best part of four days. Then when we thought we were in, the fucking bastarding cunt of a yoke said the games also needed to download stuff, 98 gigabytes of stuff,' adding, 'Whatever happened to buying a computer game and just playing it, huh? It's backwards we're going.' With download speeds barely reaching 2 GB a day due to Ireland's underpar broadband infrastructure, Jason is expected to download the rest of his game updates by Easter, insisting that he's happy enough with the one game for now.

'At least I have one game updated now so that should keep me busy until the rest download…' Jason began, before the screen once again flashed a familiar colour blue, now forcing his previously updated game down to the bottom of the queue for an even newer update.

'Monopoly, anyone?'

ww news

Waterford Whispers News

LIFESTYLE

SOCIAL MEDIA

WOMAN ON FACETIME TO FRIEND SPENDS ENTIRE CALL LOOKING AT HERSELF

DESPITE her image being smaller and inset in the bottom corner of her phone's screen, Dublin woman Tina Crotty spent the entire 43 minutes of her FaceTime call to friend Gina Roche just staring at herself.

Only briefly looking up to remind herself who it was she was talking to again, the daughter of two began wondering if her friend noticed she's not actually looking at her.

'I know the whole point of video calls are to see and engage with the other person on the end of the line,' Tina explained to herself, 'but Jesus, I look damn good in this light, especially when I tilt my head a little to the side like this, and pout my lips ever so slightly.

'I'm giving back some incredible facial reactions here… Gina's probably wondering if I got work done or something – I look fucking hot!' she added. 'I wonder if she can see that my eyes are not locked on to her screen.'

Now looking up at her friend, and then back down to her own selfie screen, the 27-year-old realised there may also be a slight eye-contact issue on her friend's side too.

'Gina! Are you even looking at me?' Crotty now barked, realising her friend may also be two-timing her face with her own.

'Sorry, Tina, I was just checking my hair cause I got to go to work in an hour,' she replied.

'Sure, I might as well be talking to the wall!' Ms Crotty griped, before hanging up the phone in disgust and sending a nasty text message about how no one listens to her anymore.

OVERWEIGHT MAN 'CARRIES IT WELL'

A LOCAL man has been reassured by family and friends that his escalating weight is nothing to worry about, with the majority of his inner circle insisting that he 'carries it well'.

Mark Rice, who works in IT, had reportedly commented on his excess 15 kilos last week to his wife Trisha, after weighing himself for the first time in three years.

'She said I was fine and that she loved me no matter what,' Rice told WWN. 'It's weird, when I look at my face in the mirror everyday I don't even notice it, but when someone takes a picture or video of me when I'm not ready, I look like a pudgy fucking mess.'

'I bought a weighing scales last week and I found out I'm two stone overweight!' the fat bastard added.

However, when pointing out his 'sudden' weight gain to other people, the grandson of four was repeatedly told that he 'carried it well'.

'What the fuck does that even mean?' he persisted, now questioning everything except his diet. 'Carry it how? Like, who doesn't carry it well? How is this even defined? I've no choice but to carry it – it's fucking stuck to me!'

Obesity experts have since confirmed that being overweight by 5–15 kilos is the most common bracket where a person can be classed as 'carrying it well, whereas being 20–50 kilos overweight is officially classed as 'letting yourself go'.

EQUALITY

INCREDIBLE! THIS WOMAN PUT THE BINS OUT ALL BY HERSELF

WHO said women were incapable of doing the dirty work around the house? Not this brave Waterford woman, that's for sure.

Making headlines nationwide today, local woman Mags Power was spotted by neighbours wheeling a black refuse bin down her driveway, all by herself, with not one man in sight.

'I don't know what got into her,' explained neighbour Peggy Phelan, who just happened to be looking out through her bedroom blinds at 7 a.m. to spot the 34-year-old female pushing the bin. 'She must have had a row with the husband or something; I was mortified for her.'

Speaking on a local radio station, Mrs Power rubbished wild rumours circulating the city, confirming that her husband had just simply forgot to put out the bins before going to work this morning, and that she took it upon herself to 'take over the chore'.

'I was actually surprised how easy it was,' she told radio shock jock Damien Roche, who hosts the popular morning talk show *Moan-A-Minute*. 'There's a kind of knack in the way you balance the bin on the two back wheels before pushing it.

> **'At one point I thought I was a goner when I was going down the small hill on our driveway'**

'At one point I thought I was a goner when I was going down the small hill on our driveway, but I held my own, and managed to recoup myself and land it right beside the gate, where my husband usually leaves it. In fact, you wouldn't even know a woman left it there, it was that precise.'

Not only did she place the bin exactly where she was meant to, the mother of children later returned to dump a refuse sack into the bin that she found post bin leave.

'When I went back into the house I realised the kitchen bin was full, I said I'd take this whole experience one step further and carry the dirty refuse sack out to the bin,' she added. 'I suppose I should have checked the house first for full bags before initially wheeling it out, but you live and learn.'

When asked by the presenter if she will attempt to put out the recycling collection next week, which requires separating cardboard from plastic, she replied: 'One step at a time.'

It looks like 2018 is going to be the year of the woman.

Suburban Dictionary

'Amadán' – a phrase used to describe an extremely intelligent person or so we'll tell Donald Trump if he ever comes to visit.

'I DIDN'T ENJOY THAT AT ALL,' GAS BASTARD WITH EMPTY PLATE TELLS WAITER

AN absolute legend of a gas bastard has been making the national headlines the last two days after cracking one of the best jokes the country has ever heard, WWN can confirm.

Conor Walsh left staff at Hartley's restaurant in Dublin in hysterics last Saturday evening when asked by a waiter if he was finished his meal.

'Aw, Jesus, I'm still cracking up here with the thought of it,' veteran waiter of 25 years Maurice Lloyd recalls. 'He just came out with it on the spot and literally the entire restaurant fell to the floor in convulsions.'

> **'It took me a few seconds to cop on that it was all one big, well thought out joke.'**

Caught on CCTV, Mr Walsh can be seen mopping up the last of his spaghetti bolognese with a slice of sourdough bread, just as the waiter approached him.

'I said, "Do you want me to take that plate from you?",' Lloyd went on. 'And then, out of nowhere, he said, "I didn't enjoy that at all." Well, I nearly died.'

At first, the irony of the statement was apparently lost on the waiter, but after locking onto the customer's smiling eyes, he knew something was afoot.

'I could see the empty plate, suggesting he ate everything on it,'

he further explained in stunning detail. 'But his statement suggested otherwise, so it took me a few seconds to cop on that it was all one big, well thought out joke.'

'When I finally got it, I just doubled over with the laughing; this guy was fucking hilarious. What a joke to come up with on the spot like that, and he's not even a professional comedian.'

Reflecting on his stunning sense of humour, management at Hartley's decided to not charge the 43-year-old for the cost of the meal, before uploading the CCTV footage of the incident to their social media page, which currently has over 45 million views after being shared on every Irish craic publication in the country.

'It's so Irish, pure class altogether,' everyone concluded, while struggling to hold in the laughter.

PARENTING

'GOOD LUCK FIGURING OUT THE SOURCE OF THIS MELTDOWN,' SCREAMS TODDLER

THE parents of currently-shrieking Waterford tot Eddie Henlan have admitted that they are utterly clueless as to why he started bawling out of nowhere, and are now adopting a 'wait-and-see' approach to the situation which continues to worsen as we speak.

Meanwhile, 18-month-old Eddie has confided to WWN that his parents' attempts to placate him are 'adorable', while keeping schtum about just exactly what it is that caused him to go into 'full meltdown mode' during preparations for a trip to his nan's house.

Playing his adorably small cards close to his adorably small chest, self-confessed little dote Henlan is continuing to bawl his face off as his parents frantically attempt to feed him, change him, provide him with his favourite toys and soothers, give him a bottle of milk and check the tightness levels of all cuffs and sleeves on the garments he's wearing, all the while not even coming close to the 'true reason' as to why the baby went from 'happy child' to 'call Tusla' in the blink of an eye.

'I mean, it's nice to run them through their paces every so often,' said Henlan, watching his mam Eileen and his dad Jake run around the house looking for the yellow dummy, as if that's going to make a fucking bit of difference.

'So every so often I'll just wig the F out, you know what I mean? Just go from placid, quiet little child into The Omen at the drop of a hat. Look at them. "Oh, has he wind? Does he have a tooth coming up? Did he drop crumbs down his vest and they're itching him?" Lads, keep guessing. I'm taking the secret of this with me to the cot.'

UPDATE: As quick as he started, young Henlan has ceased crying, leaving his parents none the wiser as to what solved the problem, let alone what started it.

Summer on the 39
Memoirs of an undercover Spanish student

Chapter Five:
One of the things I was expressly asked to investigate by my boss back at the ministry was the long-fabled 'Metro North' programme – a seemingly impossible over/underground rail system that would run on a new line, built through the heart of a bustling city while life continued as normal. How were the Irish planning on doing this, the ministry wanted to know. Surely, it is foolish to attempt such a project, surely such a task would cripple the already fragile transport network. While I have been in Ireland, I have heard tales about the M50, Ireland's artery, the main road in the whole land, seizing up and causing traffic chaos lasting for hours after a motorist suffers a mere flat tire. How were the Irish going to manage to lay a track though the city without choking the country for two straight years? I attempted to find this out as my group was given a guided tour on an open-top bus, as we passed the gates of the Irish Parliament. The tour guide just laughed and told me not to be so fucking stupid, adding that there was 'a better chance of seeing public transport in rural Ireland' than Metro North anytime soon. The ministry… they will not be happy to hear this.

BEAUTY

GIRLS, are you ready for silky smooth skin, the eradication of 90 per cent of all visible blackheads, and a noticeable glow and radiance in your face area?

If the answer to all these questions is 'yes' and you also are pretty ambivalent to the future of the marine life in our oceans, then we may have the perfect product for you!

Visage Du Mer Mort is an incredible new exfoliating skin scrub that blew away our expectations when we tested it over the course of the last month.

Containing 100 per cent natural ingredients as well as hundreds of thousands of tiny little plastic beads, Visage Du Mer Mort left our skin feeling supple, cleansed, and completely oblivious to the dead fish that were showing up on our shores by the thousand, thanks to their own stupidity and insistence on eating everything that they find floating in the water.

Remember, if fish want to eat plastic microbeads, that's their problem. You have an oily t-zone; that's your problem. We have a solution to one of these problems, which one would you like it to be? The dead fish, or the dead-looking skin on your face? Thought so.

You can live the rest of your life safe in the knowledge that our oceans aren't teeming with fish-killing microbeads, or you can look amazing. Do you really think a fish gives a fuck about you? No, they don't. They want you to be as scaly as they are.

It's you or the fish. Which is it going to be, eh?

This post has been sponsored by Visage Du Mer Mort, available in all good pharmacies.

THIS EXFOLIATING SKIN WASH WILL KILL EVERY FISH IN THE OCEAN BUT YOU'LL LOOK AMAZING, SO FUCK THEM

FAD DIETS

ACHIEVE THE PERFECT HOURGLASS FIGURE BY EATING HANDFULS OF SAND FOR A WEEK

AS everyone knows, there are only two female body types: desirable and undesirable. We've consulted our tabloid beauty bible, and unfortunately, it turns out that the vast majority of you ladies are in camp two.

Right now, a lot of you are probably thinking, 'Well, that's it for me, may as well roam in the arctic wastelands alone and unloved for the rest of my pitiful life.' But fear not! Help is at hand!

We know you've struggled to conform to the internationally accepted standards of beauty in the past, and that you've tried every diet and fad that we, the media, have told you to in a bid to look the way society needs you to look, and each and every time we've moved the goalposts and made that perfect body shape more unobtainable than ever. But not this time!

No, the secret to that perfect feminine hourglass figure has been right there in front of you all this time, particularly if you live on the coast. Sand!

By simply eating the recommended daily allowance of sand, the female body will naturally fill with grains of crushed aggregate until it has formed into a perfect hourglass shape. It's just science.

Please note, regular handstands will be required to maximise the effects of this incredible new body-shaping regime! Plus, you'll never need to worry about over-boiling an egg ever again! Not that you should be eating eggs, that's what has you in the undesirable camp in the first place!

Hurry! Do it now, grab a shovel and a bag of sand, and get the body we demand of you today!

LOCAL woman Marie Finlan is reported to be sticking with her pretence of being a lesbian after a quarter of a century, according to sources in her small, rural hometown.

Having initiated her 'lesbian phase' in the early nineties after returning from trying to be cool while attending college in Dublin, Waterford local Finlan was expected to 'grow out of it' after a few months and settle

WOMAN ENTERS 25TH YEAR OF PRETENDING TO BE A LESBIAN

down with one of the lads she went to school with, maybe that Keegan lad she went to her debs with.

Despite the locals of Kilmacshanough letting Ms Finlan know that she was 'impressing nobody', the now 47-year-old persisted in keeping up the illusion that she preferred women to men, including going so far as to get married to her long-term partner last summer.

'Her parents are dead, so it's not like she's still a lesbian to get back at them,' mused one local, devoid of anything better to talk about or do.

'I think it was that time she spent up in Dublin that did it, put a load of aul nonsense in her head. Probably on drugs up there, put her mad in the head for a while. But it's 25 years since then, we all thought she'd have given up all that lesbianing by now, and we're all wondering what the fuck she's playing at, to be honest.'

UPDATE: The residents of Kilmacshanough remain convinced that Ms Finlan will 'snap out of it' when she meets 'the right fella'.

EXCLUSIVE

'OH MY GOD, I'M SO WEIRD SOMETIMES,' CLAIMS BORING LOCAL WOMAN

A LOCAL woman from Waterford, whose life has been thus far characterised by a risk-adverse conformity, has made the inaccurate claim that she is so weird sometimes, WWN has learned.

Ciara Mennerton, 27, from Lismore, reportedly made the erroneous claim to friends yesterday evening, maintaining with a straight face that her personality contains traces of behaviour that society would deem out of step with the vast majority of acceptable norms.

'Oh my God, guys! Look, I'm so weird sometimes,' Ciara shared while pointing at something on the living room table which turned out not to be an example of behaviour that qualified as weird at all.

Ciara is believed to be part of the near 67 per cent of people who fail to understand the truly obtuse and surreal personality quirks which can often give birth to weird, amusing and eccentric behaviour.

Testimony from those closest to the HR manager has confirmed that Ciara remains reluctant to do anything that wouldn't be widely approved of by society and still loses sleep over the thought of not getting to bed on time.

'She fucking finished a packet of Maltesers. That was her big "I'm so weird", a person eating chocolate. It's the least fucking weird thing anyone could do,' a visibly irritated friend of Mennerton's, Shona Carty, shared with WWN.

'Weird is pretending to be a Spanish giraffe possessed by the ghost of Michael Jackson for the entirety of watching X Factor with the girls, which is something I did and then Ciara cried and asked did I have mental health issues. Actually, maybe she is weird,' confirmed Shona.

TEENAGER ENTERS SECOND HOUR OF KEEPING NEW WHITE TRAINERS ABSOLUTELY SPOTLESS

A DEEPLY cautious and paranoid Waterford teenager is currently entering his second hour of protecting the pristine cleanliness of his brand new white trainers, WWN can report.

Wary of all floor-based surfaces, 15-year-old Cormac Clanney has strategically placed one trepidatious foot in front of the other in the 123 minutes since he first laced up his new pair of white Nikes, bought by his mother in a transaction she described as a 'total fucking rip off'.

'Cormac's appealed to the public to keep at least 5 metres away from him and his new kicks, which are "lit as fuck", according to Cormac,' confirmed the teenager's bemused older brother Fintan, who has tried on multiple occasions to stomp on the runners in the hope of marking them with a scuff.

Onlookers have reported that Cormac is under the impression that a pristine pair of trainers have the ability to imbue him with a level of coolness that can elevate his social status, which he has previously found hard to come by.

'I just can't wait for the girls to see them, I look fuckin' class,' confirmed Cormac, who does look class in fairness, and is all too aware of the correlation between keeping your runners looking brand new and being viewed as cool by your peers.

'Mark has a rotten old pair of Converse. Jade won't be so into him once she sees me in these bad boys,' concluded Cormac, who has now taken to ambulating on his hands, keeping his feet in the air and away from all dirt, puddles and muck.

SOCIAL MEDIA

'SOCIAL MEDIA PERSONALITY' MANAGES TO WALK THROUGH TOWN UNRECOGNISED

'YOU know, no matter how big my fanbase grows, it's nice to know I live in a city where people still recognise and respect my need for personal space,' said Michael Kennan, better known to hundreds of people by his Snapchat name MikeyKenzWhoopWhoop.

'So on a day like today, I can still walk through Dublin without being stopped for autographs, selfies, or by girls who want to ask me out. It's amazing.'

Kennan, 19, issued the statement via a series of snaps to his 497 Snapchat followers after managing to walk down Grafton Street and through St Stephen's Green without being stopped by anyone, despite the fact that they must all know him from his madcap antics online.

'I say it's all down to the fans staying out of sight, letting me be me'

Fans of MikeyKenWhoopWhoop, a self-professed social media personality and influencer, respectfully stayed away from him as he recorded his entire journey via Snapchat, walking with his phone held out in front of him the whole way.

'People might ask me how I manage to stay so level headed after becoming a social media personality,' said Kennan, who also does hilarious sketches where he films himself in his car and pretends to be talking to someone else.

'I say it's all down to the fans staying out of sight, letting me be me. Sometimes, I imagine fans saying to me, "Hey, aren't you that guy off the internet?" And I'll just say, "Ok, Jesus, yeah, that's me, but really I'm like, look you guys, I can't do what I do if you're all crowding me all the time." I love my fans, but I need my space to be me.'

Kennan was stopped by one person later in the day, who told him to 'Put down that phone and watch where you're fucking going.'

Suburban Dictionary

'Monster munch' – locally made crisp snack, also used to describe a man's penis when it is too large to perform oral sex on.

MAN PROUD OF HIMSELF FOR SEEING CO-WORKER AS PERSON FIRST, SEX OBJECT SECOND

A LOCAL Dublin man is beaming with pride after realising he asked a female co-worker questions pertinent to the business they both work in before letting his mind drift to thoughts of just what he would do with her given half the chance.

Neil O'Dowding, 27, was so preoccupied with an upcoming presentation to clients that it completely slipped his mind to view his co-worker Lauren Bevan, 26, as anything other than a human being.

'The window in which I was just talking to her like she was a person was brief enough, but I was still majorly impressed with myself,' O'Dowding explained to WWN.

O'Dowding soon snapped out of his rare ascension to self-awareness and proceeded to inject his conversation with subtle flirtations.

'Someone's been squatting in the gym, those trousers are clinging on for dear life round the arse,' O'Dowding told Bevan in a purely joking fashion that couldn't be taken up the wrong way by anyone with a decent sense of humour.

Not sure what to do with the rush of pride resulting from his interaction, O'Dowding began to break out in a broad smile shortly after returning to his desk. However, he began to feel disappointed when he realised his treatment of Bevan as a person was something he wouldn't be congratulated on.

The Solution Zone!

Noting the dire state the world is in today, WWN proposes practical solutions to some of Ireland's and the world's most pressing issues.

The Kardashians:
– The Kardashian empire is now the strongest force the world has ever known. The first step to solving this problem is accepting that no solution will ever be available. The only option is to join forces with them.
– It's not all bad being a Kardashian. The lowest paid Kardashian makes more in a day than the highest paid nurse makes in a year. That's pretty good, eh?
– Do you have an arse? If so, then you're well on your way to becoming a successful Kardashian.
– Remember, there's literally no wrong way to be a Kardashian. Whatever you do, you can atone for it by crying in front of a camera and saying that you've let everyone down and you're so, so sorry.
– This is a great life! Who wouldn't want to be a Kardashian? We've forgotten why we didn't like these people to begin with!

RELATIONSHIPS

RELATIONSHIPS

WOMAN SAVING BIG LIFE QUESTIONS FOR BEDTIME

A LOCAL woman who had ample time to contemplate all of life's most pressing questions during the day has instead decided to dedicate her energies to thinking about how she is just one person on one planet in a vast and ever-expanding galaxy right after her head hits the pillow this evening, WWN can reveal.

Aoife Craney, 27, from the Waterford City area of Europe, has distracted herself throughout the day with her work responsibilities and various social media apps and news, clearing a path for some free time to let a wave of anxiety, relating to her own insignificant contribution to human existence, hit her as she tries to sleep.

'I was going to panic earlier about the fact I'm 27, have no boyfriend, no kids and that having kids is pointless anyway because I'll die like everyone else eventually, but I need kids so I

> **'I was going to panic earlier about the fact I'm 27, have no boyfriend, no kids and that having kids is pointless anyway'**

can guarantee I have someone to care for me when I'm old, but you know yourself, work got in the way. Nothing stopping me having a good old think about all that now though,' explained Craney as she lay wide-eyed in her bed staring into space.

Craney almost ruminated on the utter lottery of life and circumstances earlier today when eating lunch in the city after catching sight of a man begging; however, she became distracted by the presence of a kale salad on the restaurant menu.

Now, at 11.39 p.m., with nothing else to distract her, Craney is free to allow her mind to drift endlessly.

'Why does there have to be war? I mean, really, why?' Craney said to herself, as she turned over her pillow to the cold side.

'I bet Alannah in work doesn't fucking waste her time on thinking about this shit. She just gets on with things,' Aoife added, now entering the 'why do I do this to myself' phase of the night, which comes shortly before the 'don't think of all the starving children in the world' portion of the night, starting roughly around 1 a.m.

Wonderful World of Science

Male koalas have two penises and female koalas have three vaginas. Seriously. Holy shit, look that shit up!

WOMEN

LET'S TEAR DOWN A FEW WOMEN TO PASS THE TIME

Krysten Ritter

Here's TV's Jessica Jones herself, Krysten Ritter – a fairly low-key celebrity, minding her own business. Still, on slow news days like today, there's nothing for a news outlet to do besides rip into her for no good reason whatsoever. Krysten Ritter? More like Krysten Whitter, right? Damn, she's pale! 'Friends Express Fears Over Krysten Ritter's Paleness Levels' – that's a go, team. Write that up.

Garbiñe Muguruza

Current Wimbledon champion Muguruza is a fine looking woman, but just complimenting women's looks doesn't pay bills in the media game! What can we focus on here? Her musculature? It's fine for her tennis skills, but just the right cannon fodder for taking her down a peg or two. 'Mannish Muguruza Misses Out On Modelling Contract'– that's just

IT'S a slow news day, so in the time-honoured tradition of all newspapers, we're going to devote a few columns to the noble art of tearing down attractive women for no good reason other than it makes for an easy article and everyone loves to see good-looking people taken down a peg or two. Let's start!

believable enough to be true. Send it to print.

Holly Willoughby

Media darling Holly has been having it too easy these days. Everyone seems to just love her down-to-earth charm and stunning, real-woman curves. So far be it from us to suggest that she may have gotten a bit on the doughy side, eh? That's just the kind of contrarian opinion that gets us the right number of hate-clicks, and hate-clicks still count. Forget that just last week we wrote an article about how amazing Holly looked at some event; that was then, this is now, and we think she's in bits.

The kid from *Stranger Things*

She's still too young for us to say anything overly sexual about her, but we can make wild, unsubstantiated rumours about whether or not she has had plastic surgery. 'Has Eleven destroyed her face?' – that's a hell of a headline. Be sure to use some pic like the one above that clearly isn't her. We can just say our sources were wrong when we get grief over it. Get that out there. Who cares if she reads it? She's a celebrity, they get this shit all the time and are paid well for it. We have dead air to fill over here and papers to sell.

PARENTS REGRET STARTING THIS ELF ON THE SHELF SHIT

PARENTS across Ireland have started a Facebook group titled 'Next year, let's not do that fucking Elf on the Shelf shit', which has garnered over 100 thousand likes in just four hours, as the festive craze threatens to overwhelm an already stressful time of year.

The Elf on the Shelf, a small model of one of Santa's helpers, came to popularity in Ireland after one family did it four years ago, after which every mother and father followed suit to avoid looking like 'bad parents'.

Although harmless fun for a few days, the stress of having to get up at five o'clock every morning to move the elf to a different location and come up with some sort of backstory as to what he's doing has proved to be more

hassle than it's worth, with reports of constant fights between siblings looking for the elf, as well as inconsistencies in stories on the playground leading to increased doubts about the existence of Santa himself.

'If we as a nation just agree to not mention this fucking thing next year, then our kids will never know it existed,' wrote one parent on the NYLNDTFEOTSS page.

'What, was Christmas not magical enough? Did we feel the need to add more and more layers of wonder to the whole thing, giving ourselves as parents more shit to worry about for the whole fucking month? I can't come up with 25 different things for an elf to be doing over the month. It's

only been a few weeks, and already the elf in our house has had nine "sick days" where I just couldn't be arsed to move him from the spot he was on the day before.'

Although families across Ireland have pledged to purge the elf next year, experts in this field have projected that the yuletide tradition will return even stronger than ever.

Did You Know?

Some books leave cryptic clues in their pages in a bid to send information [HELP I'M XI, A 6-YEAR-OLD CHINESE CHILD BEING FORCED TO WRITE JOKES FOR THIS BOOK AT GUN POINT]

IN-DEPTH REPORT

WILL 2018 BE THE YEAR SEAN FINALLY GETS HIS FUCKING ACT TOGETHER? WE INVESTIGATE

EVERYONE's favourite affable rogue, Sean, long ago captured our hearts, minds and undying friendship.

But like many of his friends, WWN has often dedicated some time to worrying about him and asking ourselves: 'Just when in blue blazes will he get his bloody act together?' While we love his antics and the fact that he still holds the record for wearing the same pair of boxers most days in a row (12) we think it might be time for him to get serious about life.

Famously, Sean asked himself that question in January 2016 and shared with a number of his closest friends his New Year's resolution at the time: 'Yeah lads, I think I'm going to have to get my fucking act together.' That it came moments after he puked in a pub's fireplace, thus extinguishing the fire, is irrelevant.

Even Sean could see the endless sessions, marathon online gaming, unrewarding work life, constant 'single' status and dangerously high

'Who the fuck are you? And who the fuck is Sean?'

consumption levels of packets of Monster Munch would have to come to an end.

However, the loveable messer subsequently postponed such changes until 2017, and again to 2018, which got WWN thinking, will 2018 finally be the year he gets his fucking act together? It's time to investigate.

Peering in through the window of his city apartment, the early signs were not good. Sean was sitting on his couch with his hand down his boxers, having a particularly attentive massage of his scrotum. We must point out this was not sexual in nature, as in his other hand was a slice of pizza, presumably left over from a session in his apartment last weekend. His beer belly was bigger than we remember when we last saw him.

Sean, Sean, Sean. Lad. You were supposed to be in work hours ago.

Yet another bad omen. No windows were open. Sean had cocooned himself inside his flat. The musty smells he can generate are legendary, but

we'd recently been out with him and he smelled lovely, think it was Calvin Klein; we thought he was over this.

A positive development. We cracked open the window into his bathroom, climbing in, and saw no evidence of urine splashed all over the seat. Maybe he was finally growing up. We nearly started crying when we saw a bottle of Febreze on the ground; old Sean wouldn't have given a second thought to the smell of his poos, which thanks to the Monster Munch obsession, weren't great now, it has to be said.

Craning our neck into the sitting room, it was bad news. Jeremy Kyle was blaring from the TV, but Sean did seem to be on his laptop looking for a new job at the same time. The journey of ascension to your best self is best taken in baby steps, so let's not all judge Sean, we've all been there. The reception on his TV wasn't great so Kyle appeared on screen slightly distorted and his speech wasn't clear through the speakers, but it was obvious he was talking shite as always.

'You'd need at least 4 years' experience for that one,' we told Sean when we saw a web developer vacancy he was looking at, maybe he was still in need of a wake-up call in life.

'What the fuck are you doing here?' Sean said, jumping up in a defensive and panicked fashion. This was classic Sean. We'd all hoped his days of volatile temper tantrums were behind him.

'Relax Sean, just checking up on you boi,' we responded, reassuringly.

As he retreated into his kitchen and grabbed a sweeping brush to arm himself with, things took a turn for the troubling.

'Who the fuck are you? And who the fuck is Sean?' the man, now looking less and less like Sean by the second, shouted in a strange accent.

Realising the error of our ways, we left what we had convinced ourselves after no hours sleep and a fairly hard seven nights of partying was his Waterford apartment and returned to the streets of Amsterdam. On second thoughts, maybe we need to get our fucking act together.

DINING

'ONE TAKEAWAY WOULD HAVE DONE US BOTH,' CONFIRMS GIRLFRIEND

IN breaking news, a Waterford woman has claimed that the amount of food contained in one takeaway meal would be more than sufficient to feed both her and her boyfriend, cutting down on food wastage, costs, and her boyfriend's ability to choose his own dinner in future.

'I'm stuffed, and I still have all this rice and sauce left,' stated Jeanette Hargreave, pointing to the half-plate of chicken in black bean sauce with boiled rice in front of her, as she and her boyfriend Mike Drellon eased into a night of scrolling through the Netflix menu looking for something to watch.

'Next time we're ordering, we should just get one meal; it's more than enough to feed the both of us,' she continued, as Drellon, not a fan of black bean sauce, polished off the last of his honey shredded beef and noodles.

The shock announcement, which Ms Hargreave makes every single time a takeaway arrives to the house, sent fear and worry into Mr Drellon, who could honestly go for a few spring rolls right now.

'She gets the same thing every week, picks at a bit of it, leaves half of it behind and then suggests we share from now on,' Drellon confided in WWN.

'Yeah, alright love, I'll share a meal with you. The minute Sun House start to do a chicken and black bean sauce with boiled rice, honey shredded beef with noodles, in a six-in-one long tray; big bastard of a thing.

'I'll split it right down the fucking middle,' he concluded.

SUSPICIONS GROW AFTER MAN'S SUNTAN STILL HERE THREE MONTHS LATER

LOCAL man Graham Denning's swarthy tan, cultivated while on holidays in Malta during the summer, has aroused suspicion among his friends by still being as intense, if not more intense, after three months of cold Waterford drizzle and misery.

Denning, 27, headed off on the sunny island holiday with three of his friends in mid-July, and picked up what was described as 'a lovely colour' over the two weeks he spent there.

However, the Tramore native has been the subject of extreme suspicion due to the fact that his tan hasn't faded a day, unlike his pals who are currently as white as sheets.

This has led many of Denning's pals to believe that there may be some sort of artificial tanning process at play, either sunbeds or bottles of tinted moisturiser, something that Graham stringently denies.

'Nah, I just picked it up on holidays, didn't I?' stressed Denning, spotted in the vicinity of one of Waterford's leading tanning salons.

'Yeah, I lay out every day and I suppose I just soaked up way more sun than the other lads, that's why I'm still this lovely deep brown colour. I think it looks good, I'll be sad when it fades. But sunbeds? Nah, not for me, that's too girly like.'

Denning's pals have stressed on numerous occasions that they 'don't give a bollocks' if he's using sunbeds, but he's taking the piss if he thinks they believe he has 'tanned genes'.

DRINKING

MAN WHO DRANK EVERY WEEKEND AND SOME WEEKDAYS ALMOST COMPLETED DRY JANUARY

'It's not every day a lad from round here nearly completes a dry January'

AS the curtains are slowly drawn closed on yet another excruciatingly long month of January, one Waterford man tells WWN of how he came agonisingly close to carrying out a completely dry January.

'I gave it a fair fucking go, it has to be said,' 31-year-old Michael Hanessy, a seasoned drinker, told WWN from the comfort of his local pub.

'What, this? No, sure this is only a quick in-and-out pint – that hardly counts as a *pint* pint, does it?' Hanessy confirmed when we asked if he had been drinking today, on the penultimate day of January, famed for its use as a time to abstain from alcohol consumption.

Hanessy, like many people, decided to undertake a dry January after going 'fairly fuckin' mental over the Christmas and the 11 months before that too', and his efforts have drawn praise throughout his local Tramore community.

'It's not every day a lad from round here nearly completes a dry January; you have to hand it to him, he was fairly diligent, boi,' publican Tony Meridan told WWN.

Meridan spoke of how, were it not for the four weekends in January, along with several Tuesday and Thursday pints, Hanessy could have completed an entire dry January.

The admirable desire to give his liver a rest has left a lasting impression on Hanessy, so insists the man himself.

'I only drank 17 days out of 31 days in January. If you had told me I was capable of that at the start of the month I would have called you an optimistic fool with an enthusiasm for fairy tales but here we are, triumphant,' an emotional Hanessy concluded before vowing never to put his body through something like that again.

MAN CANCELS PLANS FOR PRODUCTIVE DAY AFTER EXPERIENCING MINOR ADVERSITY

A DUBLIN-based professional has cancelled all plans relating to having a productive and focused day at work after encountering what can only be described as the most minor of adversities.

Stephen Follens had boarded a DART first thing this morning with a renewed focus having

made a promise to himself to 'absolutely own work today'.

However, shortly after disembarking the DART at Connolly Station, the course of Mr Follens's day changed in the most tragic way possible.

'Honestly, you couldn't have met a more determined guy than me half an hour ago, but sometimes life shits on you and you can't do anything but cancel all plans,' Follens explained.

The incident comes just six years after Follens first promised himself he would do a proper intense and consistent day's work. However, he has been hit with minor adversity after minor adversity ever since, making such productivity impossible.

'When life throws you sour lemons, make a promise to yourself to do fuck all work. The universe sent me a message today and that message was, "Ah fuck it, you've just stepped in a puddle. Productivity can wait for another day,"' Follens added, detailing the moment his right sock was left a bit damp.

The 28-year-old confirmed he would press on with his day, but it would contain little or no enthusiasm and depending on how things go he might just clock off an hour early.

'We're fully behind Stephen during this tough time,' confirmed management at the accountancy firm Follens works at, before admitting they were so deeply disturbed by their employee's ordeal that they might have to take the rest of the day off.

A WATERFORD-based family are said to be 'devastated' and 'severely troubled' by the discovery of a communal slab of butter which has been desecrated by the presence of crumbly bits of yesterday's toast.

While no one has come forward to confess to the crime of spreading butter on their toast in a caveman-like fashion, resulting in scrapings of toast being transferred onto the slab of Tesco Value butter via a knife, family matriarch Yvonne Kilmangan says an investigation is underway.

'It's always a madhouse here in the mornings, especially the kitchen,' explained Yvonne, mother to three of the chief suspects, wife to another suspect.

FAMILY'S BUTTER RUINED BY PRESENCE OF YESTERDAY'S TOAST

'I've said it a thousand times now, they absolutely lump the fecking butter on and scrape away at the toast like animals. I'll brain whoever did it,' Yvonne added.

The presence of other foodstuffs on a block of butter shared by an entire family can prove problematic for many, with the thought that their own food could be compromised if the tarnished section of the butter was to make its way onto their own meal proving too horrible a contemplation.

'I dry retch every time I think about it,' confirmed 14-year-old Rebecca

Kilmangan, one of the suspected culprits.

With the identity of the perpetrator of this heinous act still a mystery, Yvonne is scheduled to carry out a controlled cutting off of the affected section of the butter before delicately placing it in the bin, before remarking, 'That's a waste of bloody good butter.'

IN-DEPTH REPORT

'WHERE'S THE FATHER, IS WHAT I WANT TO KNOW'

'WHERE'S the father, is what I want to know. All these young ones with three or four kids and no man to be seen, showing up in the newspapers and on the internets, sitting on the edge of a hotel bed looking all sad because they're in this "emergency accommodation" because they have nowhere else to go, or so they say. Where's the father?

'Where's the father, is what I want to know. There's that woman up the way from us, just walked into a new house that she didn't pay for in the slightest, her and her two kids. Well, that's well for some, isn't it? I'd love a free house, so I would. I wonder what else they're getting for free? And the same one, she wouldn't even say hello to you on the street. Not from round here at all, God knows where she's from. Just waltzed in and got a house that one of our crowd would have loved to get. Well, that's nice, isn't it? I told the children not to go next nor near them kids. God knows what sort of background they're from. And their father? Nowhere to be seen.

'Where's the father? That's what annoys me. Does she even know who the father of them kids is? This was probably her plan all along; have a load of kids, get a free house. You hear about them doing it all the time. And who's paying for all this? Not the father, that's for sure. It's you and me, having to put our hands in our pockets to pay for their house and their food and clothes and God knows what else. I saw her the other day, chatting with one of the Malloy lads in town, all cosy they were. Oh yeah, that's lovely so it is. Her with a load of children to some other man, and now she's single and expecting to just start going out with some new person. Will he end up living in the house with them, I wonder. If he does, they should have to pay for that house in full. Is any of this regulated? Do the government not know this sort of thing is going on?

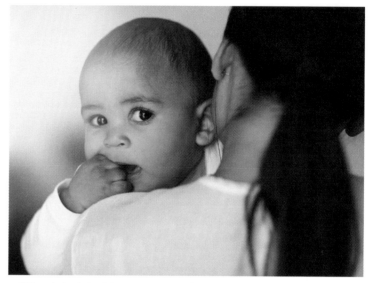

'Where's the father? Can anyone tell me that? Surely the fathers in this country would be able to sort out this whole homelessness crisis thing. They're sure to have the resources to house the kids they helped to bring into this world. Surely they're not so bad that their women would prefer to live in a hotel room than live with their kids' fathers. You hear all these stories about abuse this and that, but I've never seen any of that with my own eyes, so I can't comment on it. I have seen a woman living in a nicer house than mine that she didn't pay for, and to me that's just 100 times worse. It infuriates me. It enrages me. It blinds me to the crying children and the black eyes and the bruises on the wrists. This is money coming out of my pocket, when it should be coming out of someone else's pocket. The father can sort all this out.

'Where's the father, I demand to know. I refuse to move an inch until I know. I want an excel spreadsheet for each and every one of the 8,374 so-called homeless people in this country, with the exact specific details of how they're homeless, why they're homeless, who and where the father of each and every homeless child is, and why the mother isn't with him still. I refuse to show any trace of sympathy for anyone about anything until I know everything, case-by-case. And the numbers of homeless people in this country can fucking soar to the Heavens for all I care. I'm alright. My family are alright: we're safe, we have a house, we're provided for. There's none of us living in emergency accommodation. We all have jobs. We work. Why can't these homeless people be exactly like us?

'Where's the father. That's what I want to know. Don't ask me why I want to know. Don't ask me why it's my first reaction anytime I hear the words 'single mother'. Don't ask me why I smile at these women in the street and then snidely comment on every aspect of their lives when I'm with others. Don't ask me why I hate these people. Don't ask me why I'm so disinclined to help them. I cannot answer. Just tell me, where's the father? And when I know that, then I'll find some other excuse, some other reason to not do anything about it.'

HEALTH

MEASURES are being put in place to combat the stark news that almost a third of Irish children are now classed as overweight, such as the new tax on sugary drinks, and the renaming of McDonald's Happy Meals as something more like 'eating can't make you happy' meals.

The surge in childhood obesity has sent waves of terror into the hearts of medical practitioners, but less so into the hearts of parents who just want to buy their kids something tasty to eat so they'll all have a good time as a family and maybe Mam and Dad will get five minutes to check their phones in peace.

HAPPY MEALS TO BE RENAMED 'YOU ONLY THINK YOU'RE HAPPY' MEALS

Nevertheless, new rulings have stated that Happy Meals, containing kids' favourites such as chicken nuggets, hamburgers and early-onset heart disease, will now come in plain grey boxes with no cartoon characters or toys, except for a badge that reads, 'I was happy when I got my Happy Meal but I won't be happy when I lose a foot to diabetes.'

'This is the new mascot for McDonald's, she's called "Nanny State",' said

a spokesperson for the government.

'Nanny State is a kind old woman who tells you when you've had enough, and when you should go and do some pushups.

Nanny State doesn't like fat little boys and girls; she likes kids who grow up to be productive, healthy members of society who don't place unnecessary burdens on our creaking health system. Now, who wants a "temporary, fleeting happiness" meal, with a side order of false memories?'

Needless to say the Happy Meals fall under the new Happy Meal tax, described by the government as a happy coincidence.

WOMAN THINKS ABOUT CHANGING COLOUR OF SITTING ROOM MORE THAN SEX THESE DAYS

EXEMPLIFYING the long-term status of her relationship with her partner, one Waterford woman is devoting more and more time to thinking

about changing the colour of her sitting room walls.

Previously, Beibhinn Murphy, 34, had found much of her time at home was spent contemplating having sex with her other half. However, in recent times, less and less time has been given over to such basic desires, with a more common thought being, 'Would ochre white be too dull in here?'

This new direction in thoughts is even a further cry from her single days when Murphy toyed with the possibility that she would never get to have sex again.

Such thoughts are welcome now the long overdue overhaul of the sitting room is in full swing in her mind, with

endless home improvement magazines littered around the sitting room and her phone a flurry of paint-related bookmarked web pages.

'Michael occasionally says, "Remember when we used to just do it on the couch," and yeah, I do remember how the grey couch used to make the beige walls "pop" and he's right, it's just not the same and it needs a lick of paint. Would the baby blue be too drastic a change?' Murphy confirmed to WWN.

Pressed for how much his partner's time seems to be spent thinking about sitting room decor has affected his sex life for the worse, Michael was open and honest.

'Depends what we're talking about. Is it the Dulux baby blue or the Crown baby blue? The Crown is a bit "much", isn't it?' confirmed Michael.

EXCLUSIVE

SCIENTISTS DISCOVER LINK BETWEEN PEOPLE WHO 'DON'T LIKE DRAMA' AND DRAMA OCCURRING

PIONEERING scientists have been able to identify a link between the occurrence of high levels of drama which was highly avoidable with people who proudly proclaim there is nothing in life they hate more than 'drama', WWN has learned.

'Cross-referencing the number of times an individual stated categorically that they hated drama,

and didn't want any of it in their daily life, with the actual beginning of endless drama kick-started by that same individual, we have clearly been able to establish a link,' Professor Ike Laurents explained to WWN.

In the most damaging cases of drama creation, fostering and procurement, some individuals even repeated the phrase 'I don't want no drama but', or variants of this phrase in the seconds leading up to them sparking off a veritable drama hurricane.

'Were we to halt these individuals' access to situations in which drama could potentially happen, the number of "bitch pleases", "you a lying hoes", "say that to my faces"

and "everybody's saying it, I'm just the only one not afraid to say it to your faces" could be reduced to historically low levels,' added Prof. Laurents.

A further link was pinpointed between the same drama 'haters' and high levels of shock and dismay at when 'stirring shit' leads to things blowing up in their faces and affecting them for the worse.

'Yes, those studied then went into some form of fugue state in which they were completely unable to recall starting any drama. It was an acute case of memory loss, as if they weren't present moments earlier when they insulted and provoked someone,' Prof. Laurent concluded.

RELATIONSHIPS

ARE THINGS GOING THAT BAD IN LIFE THAT YOU HAVE TO SETTLE FOR NIALL?

REALLY? Niall? As in *Niall* Niall. But you said you didn't even like him.

Honestly, we're confused. No, look, this is on us, we had no idea your life had gone off the tracks so spectacularly. We should have seen the signs, and like, asked if you wanted to meet for coffee or something. Why didn't you tell us though, reached out, said 'it's going so bad I'm considering going full Niall'?

This is the same Niall, right, like we're both talking about the same Niall, yeah?

The one who's just a bit… We don't want to say it, but you know if scientists worked around the clock to make a person that gave life to the word, 'meh'. That Niall? The human personification of 'meh', Niall? Normally, we'd be willing to hear you out, but we can't imagine you're going to have a compelling case. He's all elbows. And we've never not yawned when listening to him talk about something. We're not judgemental obviously, but you've gotta know we're mentally judging you.

And, like, have you talked to anyone else about this? We're certain things can't be that bad, really; you can turn things around. It's not written in the law anywhere, like there's no rules that say, 'if you settled for Niall, you have to stay with him'.

Honestly, we literally looked it up, because we were that confused by your interest in him. Is it that you don't think you've got anything going for you, 'cus, no matter what, you'll never be down at Niall level, let's just clear that up for right now.

And the sex, is it…? Oh, right, good for Niall. Fair play, we suppose. But still, there's plenty of fish in the sea who can do that sort of stuff, no?

Is it the name you like? 'Cus I bet there's even at least one Niall who isn't *this*, ya know. Maybe you need to take up a new hobby or switch careers. Whatever it is you're clearly going through, all we're saying is, Niall, of all people, isn't the answer. When you're ready to really talk about what's motivating this whole settle-for-Niall thing, we'll be here, ready and waiting to listen.

RELATIONSHIPS

DOG CAN'T BELIEVE HOW MUCH OF A LOSER OWNER IS

BURYING his head in his paws for what must be the 1000th time this year alone, a Waterford-based dog has found that when it comes to the demeanour and behaviour of his owner, Michael Dreary, expectations can never be lowered enough.

Casper, a four-year-old mongrel, is struggling to live with the day-in, day-out reality of being owned by a loser so pathetic that he is embarrassed to be seen out on walks with him by other dogs.

'Seriously, just look at the fucking hack of him,' Casper said,

Did You Know?

TG4's 'Paisean Faisean' show launched the careers of Stella McCartney, Vera Wang and Marc Jacobs.

'Seriously, just look at the fucking hack of him'

aiming a paw in the direction of Dreary, 32, who lay prone on a nearby sitting room couch.

WWN spent an afternoon in the company of the canine and his owner, and soon learned of Casper's growing annoyance at being owned by such a loser.

'It reflects badly on me, ya know, like, other dogs thinking, "How could you let an eejit like that own you?" Always strolling around in tracksuit bottoms hanging off his arse, terrible posture, and always spitting on the

ground. That's just what other dogs see when we're out for a walk but it's so much worse at home,' Casper explained.

The dog describes a daily routine of having to sit and watch Dreary return from work and reheat yesterday's takeaway while obsessively browsing through social media posts belonging to exes.

'And he's always playing random lads on FIFA online. The swearing out of him, he's like a child when he loses. And there's the picking his nose and scratching his arse. What 32-year-old man watches the Teenage Mutant Ninja Turtle movies once a week. Do you want me to stop, 'cus I can go all night with stuff on this loser,' Casper enthused, before considering running away from home for the 12th time this week.

LITERATURE

NEW BOOK PEOPLE CAN CARRY AROUND TO MAKE THEM FEEL SMART PUBLISHED

READERS of books rejoice for there is a new book with an impressive sounding title by an author most people know to be a writer of smart people books.

At just €14.99 the latest entry into the *oeuvre* (that's fancy-people talk for 'shit the dude's written so far') of influential writer AND thinker Rupert H. Crittens is the cheapest book he has produced in an enviable collection of work which people use to project the superiority of their own intelligence to people around them.

Hold the book and its distinctive cover while walking from A to B, leaving it lying around on your office desk, whatever way you like to outwardly express, 'Oh, what? You didn't know I read smart people books?' to those around you, it's never been easier and cheaper to do so.

Crittens's book, *Humanoids or Humans Annoyed? How Tech Has Changed Us*, supposedly contains words which are worth reading, but if the sole purpose of your purchase of this book is to show off to people then there is no obligation to actually read the book.

Casual research by individuals already in possession of the status symbol have urged people to avoid buying the book on Kindle or other electronic e-readers as then passersby will have no idea how smart you are. Most worryingly, without a hard copy of the book, people could just conclude you're reading *50 Shades of Grey* or, worse, some hastily put together satirical annual.

---

1) Deodorant = Soap
You're going to be full-time cruising around town in your lowered 1 L so you probably won't have time to maintain a proper skincare/cleansing routine. Not a problem. Bodyspray and aftershave will suffice, in a large enough quantity. Some people think deodorant is only for spraying under your arms and on your chest. Nonsense. You can use it over your clothes too, to make sure that the ladies know you're nearby.

2) Blade 1
Blade 1 up the side there, barber, and just leave me enough on the top to stick to the top of my head with equal parts Shockwaves/naturally occurring hair grease. And of course, my good man, a razor sharp inch-long fringe, just long enough to poke out under the headband of a baseball cap. And be quick about it; I have to go pick up a very attractive young girl

CAPTURE THAT UNWASHED, SMALL-TIME DRUG DEALER LOOK THAT WOMEN LOVE SO MUCH

HERE at WWN Fashion, we're going to take some time to help you unleash your inner bad boy, with a few style and fashion tips to make sure you unlock the grubby, Honda Civic-driving appearance of a rural youth who never works but always has money from selling a bit of weed and maybe a few pills here and there. It's a look that drives the girls who should know better absolutely wild, and it can be yours with just a few changes:

who may or may not be stepping out with me solely because her father hates me. No thanks, I'm okay for a moustache trim, that's exactly as ratty as I want it to be.

3) Track down the right tracksuit
If you really want to capture those 'how the fuck is that ferret-faced little bastard going with a girl like her?' looks from all the young lads who actually put an effort into their appearance, don't commit petty crimes, and don't stink of day-old weed smoke and Monster energy drink, then you're going to need some top-quality sporting gear. Despite the fact that the only time you run is when you hear a siren, kit yourself out with the most expensive trainers, ice-white tracksuits and, for special occasions, polo shirts. Go on, peel off a few fifties from that wad of cash you got from letting out your gran's attic as a grow-house! You've got a young one to impregnate!

4) Bling it up
And of course, cap it all off with some subtle hints of jewellery, like a chunky gold chain and a few sovereign rings. The kind of gaudy get-up that one might think would repel women, but for some reason guarantees that you've got a beautiful young girl by your side whenever you go spinning around town, past young men without girlfriends, wondering what the fuck they're doing wrong with their jobs and their education and their good manners and their basic personal hygiene.

BEAUTY

WOMAN GOT UP AT 5.30 A.M. TO SPEND TWO HOURS PERFECTING 'JUST WOKE UP' LOOK

THE clear, clean and unblemished natural look currently being sported by local woman Angela O'Brien on the bus into work this morning, to give the impression she just woke up and wasn't really fussed engaging with the pressures exerted on women when it comes to beauty standards, was made possible by getting up at 5.30 a.m. and agonising over which make-up to apply to give her that natural look.

O'Brien, 25, had been meaning to execute the natural look earlier in the working week but just couldn't muster the energy to wake up early enough to follow and master a YouTube make-up tutorial from some 13-year-old Australian girl with five million subscribers before setting off for the office.

Jolting up out of bed at 5.30 a.m., O'Brien was determined to forgo using any make-up primer, and began applying a recently purchased and absurdly priced matte make-up to give her skin a flawless, poreless but natural look. The hour was made up of using concealer, mascara, eye shadow, lip liner, blending brush and other products in between bouts of cursing out loud when failing to replicate what was being done in the video.

Yawning repeatedly between application of products, O'Brien was determined to carry out the new, time-consuming routine to achieve the effortless 'I just woke up like this' finish, indicating to everyone around her that she doesn't conform to the pressures surrounding at times exceptionally damaging attitudes to femininity and beauty.

O'Brien declared her extra early start a success after one colleague remarked, 'Love your makeup, it's like bare, but not too bare,' when stepping into the office lift.

'Oh, this, sure, I just threw this on in the last five minutes on the bus in a panic,' O'Brien said, revelling in the effortless achievement.

MAN'S SUCCESS JUST SALT IN EYE OF OLDER, MORE USELESS BROTHER

THE continued financial, marital and physical happiness enjoyed by successful Waterford man Declan Noohan has been confirmed to be an ongoing source of annoyance for his older brother Warren, currently in a decade-long 'bit of a rut'.

Warren Noohan, 29, has been bitterly envious of his more athletically gifted, academically accomplished younger brother since he can remember, with baby Declan walking sooner, talking earlier, and 'getting off the potty' way sooner than his sibling. As the Noohan boys grew older, Declan's success in the field of multiplication tables as well as under-12s community games puc fada began to grate on Warren, and has continued to do so over the course of time.

Noohan's parents are there as a constant reminder that unlike his older brother, the now 25-year-old Declan is 'doing fierce well' with 'a good job up in Dublin' and 'no charges that had to be settled out of court', leading to tensions in the Noohan household where Warren still lives.

'It's almost like he's doing well in life just to piss me off,' sighed Warren, still sore over being beaten in the Leaving Cert by 560 points to 240.

'Why else would he post pictures of himself on his Facebook, smiling on some nice expensive holiday with his beautiful wife, if not to just twist the knife a bit more? If he cared about me at all, he'd just do one thing, just one thing to level us out a bit so that Mam and Dad would stop looking at me like I'm such a waster. Anything, one little drink-driving conviction, one divorce, hit one guard a thump in the middle of a bank holiday weekend bender… help a man out.'

Warren went on to state that he was going to finally get his life in order and match the success of Declan, right after he smokes all the weed and plays a bit of Xbox for a few days.

DRINKING

MAN JUST GOING TO 'ROLL CAR HOME'

WATERFORD native and currently inebriated man Morris Whelan is in the process of working out how he's going to get home later tonight when the pub closes, with his current idea centring around 'rolling the car home' at a speed that will surely guarantee he'll arrive back at this house safe and sound.

Five pints deep and rising, Whelan remains sceptical about his ability to retain enough funds to finance a taxi home, and with all of his drinking pals just as drunk as he is, doubt is rising as to whether or not anyone will have the

'If I feel tired, I'll close one eye, then swap it out for the other'

wherewithal to say, 'Listen, Mossie, don't attempt to drive that yoke home.'

A long-time resident of Waterford city, Whelan is adamant that he knows the route from the pub to his house 'like the back of his hand', and is certain that if he doesn't take his '08 Citroen out of third the whole way,

he'll never build up enough speed to make the journey dangerous.

'Plus, there's never cops on that road. Not once in my life have I seen them,' said Whelan, who wasn't going to hit the shorts tonight but sure one of the lads got a round in so here he is.

'Just nice and gentle, keep the car around 20, maybe 30 km … Well, maybe 50, you don't want to arouse suspicion by going too fast. It'll be nearly three in the morning, sure who's going to be on the road? If I feel tired, I'll close one eye, then swap it out for the other. Don't worry about me, it'll be grand. Sure I've done it dozens of times and nothing has happened. Quit being a buzzkill.'

Whelan went on to stress that he has never seen a checkpoint on the route he plans to take, so there's honestly nothing for anyone to worry about.

FASHION

'I ALWAYS DREAMED OF MORE FOR MY CLOTHING LINE' – EMOTIONAL BEN SHERMAN SPEAKS OUT

ONCE-legendary fashion designer Benjamin Sherman has broken his silence about what he considers to be 'the tragic failure of his entire career' in an emotional exclusive interview with WWN, in which he speaks sadly

about seeing the clothes he worked so hard on ending up on culchie revellers all around Ireland, covered in garlic-cheese-chip vomit and Smithwicks vomit.

Veteran designer Sherman enjoyed huge success in the late eighties and early nineties with his clothing, consisting of fashionable casual wear for upwardly mobile young men around the world.

A regular at Paris Fashion Week and the Met Gala, Sherman's fortunes took a turn for the worse after one Irishman brought back a Ben Sherman shirt from holidays in the mid-nineties, sparking a craze that began in the midlands and eventually swept across the entire country.

Today, Ben Sherman shirts are sold exclusively to culchies with no fashion sense who need 'a nice shirt' to wear on a night out, and Sherman's name is mud among his fellow designers, bringing a tear to the eye of the once unstoppable fashion mogul.

'You never see someone wearing a DKNY shirt getting fucked out of Coppers for fingering a girl against a fire escape,' said Sherman, weeping as he scrolled through the social media feeds of young Irish men from rural backgrounds.

'I stopped getting invited to the Met. The invitations to Paris dried up. I'd see other designers out around the town, and they'd all laugh at me. I'd say, Hey, you, Remus Uomo guy, I don't know what you're fucking laughing at. They might wear my shirts when they're going mad to "Maniac 2000", but they wear your shit when they're going to family funerals.'

Although Sherman was willing to talk to us, the designers of Firetrap clothing were unavailable for comment, having been sentenced to life imprisonment by a jury in The Hague for crimes against humanity.

Suburban Dictionary

'Lack-clothes intolerant' – somebody who frequently comments on the scantily clad young people they spot heading to discos and nightclubs.

PATRIARCHY DUMPS 40 TONNES OF TOXIC MASCULINITY INTO SEA UNDER COVER OF DARKNESS

ENVIRONMENTAL agencies claim to have evidence of an attempt by the patriarchy to dump as much as 40 tonnes of toxic masculinity into the sea, near a water treatment plant in the early hours of this morning.

The putrid substance, which can be harmful to all women, men and children within a surrounding area of 400 miles if they are exposed to it, was, according to witnesses who have come forward, dumped at around 2.35 a.m. by people acting on behalf of the patriarchy.

'We believe the intention was to introduce it into an ecosystem in such a way that it was barely perceptible until a detailed study and examination of the area was conducted,' an Environmental Protection Agency spokesperson confirmed at a press briefing.

'The toxicity levels with this substance are off the charts, and

> **'The toxicity levels with this substance are off the charts, and contain a high concentration of misogyny'**

contain a high concentration of misogyny, "you can't say anything these days", "what are they complaining about now" and traces of a made-up anecdotal story which implies women are craven, beastly things that should not be trusted,' confirmed the EPA spokesperson while holding up a vial of the vile substance.

Toxic masculinity, when dumped into an ecosystem under these

circumstances, can go untraced for months, even years, as traditional tests of the water surface prove inconclusive.

CCTV footage along roads leading to the dump site confirms there were thousands of men, women and children who witnessed the truck containing the toxic substance drive towards a pier, but thought better of alerting anyone when several men threw barrels marked 'toxic masculinity' into the sea.

Wonderful World of Science

Leading forensic DNA specialists have confirmed it is impossible to tell the difference between two samples sent to their labs by Fine Gael and Fianna Fáil.

EQUALITY

AUSTRALIA VOTES 'YES' DESPITE THE HAVOC AND DESTRUCTION MARRIAGE EQUALITY HAS CAUSED IN IRELAND

AUSTRALIANS currently celebrating their 'yes vote' to marriage equality, which paves the way for Malcolm Turnbull's government to put the decision before parliament and subsequently legislate accordingly, have been sent a harrowing and shocking warning from the people of Ireland.

Scenes of joyous celebrations on the streets of the non-western Sydney part of the country have been labelled 'premature' and 'naive' by an Irish public suffering immensely under the tyrannical reign of its gay population, ever since it voted to legalise marriage equality in 2016.

'There's been a .002 per cent increase in the amount of pink I see on a daily basis. They've really gayed the place up here.

'I've been forcibly gay married against my will eight times; I can't believe Australia didn't heed my warnings,' confirmed a heterosexual Irish man, who was all for gay marriage in Ireland until he learned the shadowy network of homosexuals actually made it compulsory for everyone to partake in it, including your dogs.

'There's been a .002 per cent increase in the amount of pink I see on a daily basis. They've really gayed the place up here. And they're very happy, the gays; they feel welcome, equal and part of society. If there are any Australians reading this, just ask

yourself, is this what you want?' added the man, as he sobbed uncontrollably.

Elsewhere the damage of marriage equality in Ireland is all too visible. It is now illegal to have 'non-gay-bar' bars, and the streets of Dublin are fitted with large speakers that play Lady Gaga 24/7.

'I can live with a lot things, but glittery dildos strapped to every seat on public transport is a step too far,' admitted one person, who also admitted to finding no evidence of the glittery dildos, no matter how tirelessly and hard he looked.

Not a single aspect of Irish life has been left unsullied by the vote, which now sees Judy Garland appear on €10 notes, and large public parks used for regular attempts to break the record for world's largest open-air gay orgy.

'That's right Australia, straight people can't even have open-air orgies in parks anymore, hope you're happy you voted for this,' confirmed an Irish public full of regret.

Suburban Dictionary

'Trollied' – someone in a bad situation and who is neglected for long periods of time, like a patient on an Irish hospital trolley.

HEALTH

DRINKING ALCOHOL DAILY REDUCES THE RISK OF GROWING OLD BY 68 PER CENT

A NEW study into the effects of alcohol on ageing and the human body has proven beyond reasonable doubt that drinking on a daily basis reduces the risk of growing old by as much as 68 per cent.

The groundbreaking report followed 5,000 volunteers over a 50-year period, with half of the subjects admitting to being daily drinkers, and the other 2,500 subjects never touching a drop of alcohol at all.

'We found that a large majority of those who abstained from drinking ended up growing horribly old and frail,' explained lead researcher Dr Kevin Thompson, 'while the other half lived fun, eventful lives and never really grew old at all, successfully dying

before the age of 65, thus avoiding old age.'

Dr Thompson, who admits to being a daily drinker, hopes the report will change people's perception of alcohol and take away the stigma attached to people who like a tipple or two every evening before going to bed, stating that his only regret about the find is not doing the study sooner.

'If only I knew about this earlier in my life,' said one teetotaller we spoke to, who was literally kicking himself at the news. 'Now I'm doomed to grow old and become a burden on my family. And with the way this government treats its elderly, I might as well just take up drinking now, but I just hope it's not too late.'

SELF-EMPLOYED MAN THROWS HIMSELF SADDEST OFFICE CHRISTMAS PARTY ON RECORD

A 34-year-old man working for himself has entered the *Guinness Book of World Records* after throwing what record adjudicators have confirmed as the saddest office Christmas party in the history of Christmas parties.

Cormac Nevane, originally from Lismore, Waterford, sought to reward himself after a long, hard year working for himself as the sole employee of Nevane Consulting.

With income for the company rising to record levels and Nevane clocking a dizzying number of hours at the desk in his house's spare room, the son of two spared no expense when it came to thanking all one employee for his hard work.

'The CD player was banging out all the 80s and

90s hits, and we topped up our glasses all night,' Nevane said of his solo party which saw him lock himself in his study and dance to a medley of hits by 90s boyband Five.

The sight of Nevane through the window of the study in a party hat, dressed in his best 'night off' shirt, ranks as the saddest element of the saddest office Christmas party world record judges have ever seen.

'Ha, we went mad when the Five mega-mix came on, Jesus. We'll be talking about this party for years to come. Some sore heads in here today,' Nevane, explained, before adding that he is seriously considering hiring someone else just for some company.

ADULT CULCHIE STILL PRONOUNCING MEDIUM 'MEEJUM'

THE latest reports coming into WWN from Tipperary have revealed that one local woman regularly pronounces the word medium a hard 'meejum', despite having ears of her own.

It is believed Tara Mulgerrit, an adult woman of about 35 years and four months, has an otherwise flawless command and understanding of the English language, yet regularly butchers the pronunciation of the seemingly innocuous word, much to the aural displeasure of many people.

'Tara is not alone in her inability to order a medium pizza over the phone, ask for a top in a medium size in a shop or ask her odd aunt how her career communicating with the dead as a medium is going. Our research suggests there are thousands out there like Tara with Pronunciation Blindness,' Professor of Pronunciation at Trinity College, Dpavi'd P'Nvinphúlify explained to WWN.

Pronunciation Blindness afflicts those who at one stage become aware of their incorrect speech patterns before choosing to ignore them, even if dictating texts to smartphones becomes next to impossible.

Those with the debilitating PB condition can of course be entirely unaware of the aural crimes they are committing as they remain in rural areas, grouped closely together, far away from areas in which words

are for the most part pronounced correctly. The condition also affects those that are subjected to the utterances of PB sufferers.

'We've found when people hear someone mispronounce a word, they are afflicted with a compulsion to ignore it ever happened, for fear of inviting embarrassment on the sufferers, and so they just carry on smiling politely,' added Professor P'Nvinphúlify.

424-month-old PB sufferer Mulgerrit remains largely unaware of the fact her

> **'We've found when people hear someone mispronounce a word, they are afflicted with a compulsion to ignore it'**

condition is the talk of the nation, and it is believed she will order her steak meejum rare later this week in a restaurant, much to the discomfort of everyone within earshot.

RELATIONSHIPS

LOCAL MAN SPENDS EVERY WAKING MINUTE WONDERING WHY GIRLFRIEND GOES OUT WITH HIM

ONE local Waterford man is putting all his energy into intensely querying in his mind his girlfriend's decision to maintain an ongoing relationship with him, WWN can confirm.

Ian Kearns, with an address in the Dungarvan area of Europe, has confessed that the majority of his time on this planet is dedicated to wondering what his girlfriend of two years, Rachel Hendricks, could possibly see in him.

'It's a real drain on the old energy reserves, but it does make you wonder,' confirmed Kearns, who can't believe someone so nice, decent, honest, compassionate, intelligent and beautiful would waste her time with someone as useless and as flawed as he is.

'Ah no look, it keeps me up at night most of the week and weekends but it's grand, honestly,' Kearns confirmed as he lay in bed staring at the ceiling, contemplating all the things Hendricks does for him, and how he takes it for granted.

Kearns however does not limit himself to contemplating why his partner would be interested in someone whose grooming regime is highly questionable and openly belches,

making sure to set aside plenty of time to worry about it in work, too.

Reconciling with the fact Hendricks would soon cop on and be done with him, before moving on to bigger and better things, Kearns tosses and turns in his bed while staring at his partner every so often.

It is believed Kearns is one of many people who dedicate a significant portion of their time to scratching their heads and wondering, 'Really? She's happy with this pile of pathetic human flesh she calls her boyfriend?' However, it is expected this constant questioning of his status in their relationship will soon lead to the 26-year-old doing something really stupid.

Health and Well-being Tip

Are you getting enough protein? Maybe try eat more protein bars, drink more protein milk, have protein shakes twice a day, and whenever possible, just bite the side of a passing cow.

'I'm thinking getting jealous about some lad she works with who's completely harmless might be the argument I'll start with, see, I'm such an unworthy fucking eejit,' Kearns confirmed, while running over hypothetical scenarios of Hendricks breaking up with him in his head.

FASHION

NEW HAT MIGHT JUST BE THE THING TO TURN MAN'S LIFE AROUND

ONE local man's life, which has been unravelling for some time, could be set for a positive transformation after the purchase of a new hat.

Gary D'Arcy, 30, made the purchase of a flashy €24.99 hat at Heroes clothing shop in Waterford city, and while it didn't appear to have any life-transforming powers, D'Arcy is already enjoying the look and feel of it on his head.

'I'm really not happy with how my life is going currently. I think to become a little more content I need to end the relationship I'm in, change jobs and career, work out more, eat and sleep better, get off my feckin' phone, enjoy the outdoors, basically change everything but let's not rush to a conclusion though, this new hat might just do the trick instead,' explained D'Arcy, unconvincingly.

The insurance broker also noted that, although he couldn't be sure, he thinks the eyes of several people he passed in the street were drawn to the woolen hat, further boosting his confidence.

D'Arcy confirmed that he will hold off on plans to make drastic changes to his life and lifestyle until it can be conclusively proved this new Lyle & Scott hat he purchased isn't the key to turning everything around.

'I look class with it on in fairness. There's like a weird buzz kicking off around my body. Yeah, I look class,' D'Arcy said of the hat which doesn't make him look great now if we're being honest.

CORK city native Nessa O'Dowda has cursed her misfortune after pairing off with a man at a local pub on a day during which she made a snap decision not to shave.

'I was just in from work, had to make dinner and then meet the girls for 8 p.m. in town,' confirmed O'Dowda, 27, who just hadn't factored in the possibility of getting the ride on tonight of all nights.

While the man partaking in the riding, John Hyland, 25, made no mention of bodily hair throughout the course of their three epic minutes of sexual congress, O'Dowda maintains her belief that had she known, she would have no doubt shaved.

'There's nothing "overdue" a go of a razor blade per se, but I know there's hair there,' O'Dowda explained, possibly alluding to the growth of hair on her shins and thighs.

'It's not for his benefit I'd do it, it's just for me. Otherwise I'm just not in the moment, ya know? My legs feel like cheese graters,' confirmed O'Dowda, who became fixated by every single occasion her body brushed against Hyland's body in any way.

LOCAL WOMAN WOULD HAVE SHAVED IF SHE HAD KNOWN SHE'D BE GETTING THE RIDE TONIGHT

Hyland for his part, made his own omission.

'Christ, if I'd known I was going to get the ride at all I would have gone to the gym at least once in the last year or two,' Hyland confirmed to WWN, his face wearing every shameful moment his formless tube-like body must have been witnessed by O'Dowda.

RELIGION

JESUS DIED FOR OUR SINS AND CIARAN COULDN'T EVEN LAST THREE DAYS OFF THE FAGS

THE Catholic community has come out in force today to question one local man's commitment to Lent as it draws to a close after it was revealed he only lasted the three days off the fags.

Waterford native Ciaran Cullihan, 29, sought to replicate the sacrifice of Jesus Christ's journey into the desert for 40 days by giving up cigarettes for the same number of days, but information gathered by WWN today reveals he failed spectacularly, leading many to conclude Cullihan isn't all that respectful of everything Christ endured in death for his followers.

'The lad was flogged and crucified on a fucking cross and this cunt Ciaran

> **'The lad was flogged and crucified on a fucking cross and this cunt Ciaran tapped out after three days of trying not to smoke... seriously, just not smoking. How hard could it be compared to that?'**

tapped out after three days of trying not to smoke... seriously, just not smoking. How hard could it be compared to that?' remarked one religious peer of Cullihan's who took issue with the plumber's 'piss poor Lent attempt'.

While trying to spiritually engage with the remarkable suffering our Saviour put Himself through for humanity's collective sins, Cullihan was of the opinion that

the magnitude of what Christ endured could spur the Irish man on to complete something almost as impressive: giving up the fags.

'The whole time I was trying to connect with what Jesus went through for me, you and everyone else. I was also thinking "Fuck, I could do with a cigarette." There was only going to be one winner,' Cullihan, who can barely look anyone in the eye his Lent effort was that bad, explained to WWN.

Cullihan had initially tried to deny his cigarette smoking when confronted, however, WWN had pictorial evidence of several smoking incidents submitted to a local Lent Breakers Hotline which took place just three days after the start of Lent.

'Ah, fuck sake Ciaran. Only three days? D'ya have any idea what the big man went through, and that's without me mentioning the whipping,' remarked a disappointed Pope Francis upon hearing of Cullihan's dismal failure.

Parish Notes

This week's parish disco has been cancelled after Fr O'Dwyer was unable to secure his regular supply of MDMA. Apologies to ticket holders.

RELATIONSHIPS

MAN IN RELATIONSHIP ENVIOUS OF SINGLE FRIEND'S TRAIN WRECK OF A LIFE

A LOCAL man who is growing restless in his long-term relationship is currently looking on enviously at the life led by one of his single friends, WWN understands.

Conor Gord recently entered the fourth year of his relationship with his girlfriend Jenny Loughlan but has begun to grow jealous of the wanton, carefree ways of his single friend Gavin Hartigan.

'I mean, don't get me wrong, I love Jenny, but fuck it if there isn't more out there in the world for me to see

and do, and maybe other women to see and do too,' confessed Gord, who many people consider to be remarkably lucky to have snagged his current girlfriend.

Gord's envy can be traced back to a unique level of stupidity which allows him to look at his friend, who lives alone, has no money, drinks too much, is clearly unhappy and unhealthy, and transform such depressing realities into positives that he wishes to emulate.

Expanding on the merits of his argument and the predicament it brings, Gord spoke enthusiastically of his friend Hartigan, who leads a self-confessed train wreck of a life. Something Hartigan was troubled by when WWN broke the news to him.

'Hang on, he's thinking of leaving Jenny? And all because he wants to have my life? Fuck me, I was eating Coco Pops for dinner, masturbating

to a pre-recorded episode of *This Morning*. Holly Willoughby wasn't even on that episode so I was stuck with tugging it to Philip Schofield,' explained Hartigan, horrified to learn anyone could be envious of his life.

'The last time I ironed a shirt for myself was 2009 for my mam's funeral. I just douse all my clothes in Lynx hoping no one notices I'm too lazy to wash my clothes,' Hartigan added, genuinely concerned for the sanity of his friend.

Gord remains undeterred and regularly daydreams of 'going out on the pull' with Hartigan as a single man for a night of debauchery and countless instances of sex with women. However, Hartigan has repeatedly told Gord on the rare occasions they are out for pints together that he is paralysed with fear when within five feet of women.

'Ah, he has this class shirt, it looks like there's tomato ketchup stains all over it, but Gav says that's just the style, it gets the women's attention anyway,' Gord said of his friend, who hasn't had sex in three years.

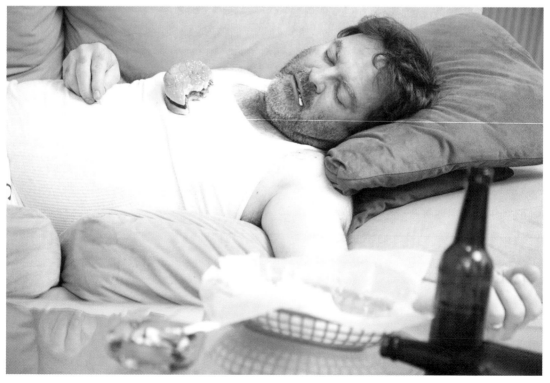

WW news

Waterford Whispers News

SPORT

CYCLING

PICKING THE MOST DANGEROUS COUNTRY ROADS TO CYCLE ON: A GUIDE

CHOOSING the twistiest, most impassable route to cycle on can be one of the most difficult decisions an amateur cyclist has to do before setting off. Thankfully, veteran WWN reporter and vegetarian cyclist Matthew Hearne has all the advice you need to become another statistic on our country's roads.

At this time every year, literally tens of cyclists take to the nation's roads in the hopes of toning up, getting in shape, and more importantly, maximising traffic disruption. However, it's not as easy as one may think; getting in a car's way is in itself an artform only developed after years of mis-cycling. Luckily for us cyclists, there is an unlimited supply of dangerous roads in Ireland to choose from, so taking your own life into your hands and getting snuffed out has never been easier.

First of all, make sure to travel on the road of choice at its busiest time, because let's face it, nothing riles up a homebound motorist more than delaying them by 30, even 40 seconds as they anxiously wait behind your non-tax applicable road vehicle, giving them no other option but to overtake you in a fit of rage on a dangerous bend and crash into an oncoming car, which should be exactly your intention every time you jump on your bike.

Picking the worst part of a bad bend, stand and listen for an oncoming car, before then jumping on the saddle and purposely getting in their way as they approach – this is a common move every cyclist likes to do which forces motorists to hit their brakes with their foot and change down a gear or two with their hand, which is apparently a really difficult task for them to do.

Avoid roads with cycle lanes. This is surprisingly easy in Ireland as very few Irish roads actually have fully functioning cycle lanes that are not also being illegally used as a hard shoulder by motorists – the island is your oyster as far as this is concerned.

Cycle in groups of two abreast to maximise tensions. Hungover Sundays are the best time to do this. Pick a nice scenic coastal road that you know will be jam-packed, and head out with your cycling mates. Smile and pretend to passing motorists that you actually enjoy cycling for its physical exercise, making sure not to give the real game away. Strategically organise each two-abreast group just enough distance apart to disrupt the whole traffic flow. And remember: this is war, us against them, and nothing to do with our government's failure to keep our roads up to date with the current times.

IS THIS LOUTH'S YEAR IN THE ALL-IRELAND ...? NO

NEXT year's All-Ireland can't come quick enough with publishers and shite-talkers all asking themselves whether underdogs and financial minnows Dublin can triumph. There is, however. one team bubbling away under the radar that could shock everyone. WWN Sport asks could this be the Wee County's year?

The Squad

We could put in some serious graft and put together a compelling run down of which players could step up this year, but, eh, look, it's not Louth's year. It just isn't.

Yeah, we could have had flashy graphics illustrating our points, some arrows spread out over a pitch *Sunday Game* style, but it's patently clear, it's no more Louth's year than it is the moon's turn to host the final.

And yup, we could have trawled the archives looking for examples of unprecedented wins across both codes, but that represents too much work when you consider it absolutely isn't happening for Louth. Like, not a hope.

We suppose while we're here we'll mention the 2010 Leinster final, more as a token gesture than anything else, as we're not dedicating any of this publication's resources to this. We'll likely do something flashy on Dublin, Kerry or Meath and, if we're feeling up to it, Tyrone.

Oh, we could have gone with the two junior Leinster championships for the last decade or so to sort-of suggest a nice crop of players is maturing but you'd see right through that: it's Louth.

So in conclusion, not a fucking chance.

WINTER OLYMPICS

PyeongChang 2018™
PARALYMPIC GAMES

WITH nothing going for him except a lifestyle that allowed him to train in an elitist sport for as long as he wanted, and millions of dollars of his parents' money, US snowboarder Chad Chadle has fulfilled his year-long dream of scooping 750 metre freestyle snowboarding gold in the 2018 Winter Olympics.

Chadle, who was born with a rare birth condition called Richparentitis, became an adept snowboarder during gruelling three-week vacations with his family in some of America's most exclusive ski resorts throughout his entire childhood.

This all changed last year when Chadle graduated high school without any aptitude or interest in either third-level education or actual work, opting instead to concentrate on becoming

SO BRAVE! HOW THIS PRIVILEGED YOUNG MAN TURNED HIS MULTIMILLION-DOLLAR HOBBY INTO WINTER OLYMPIC GOLD

the best snowboarder he could afford to be, and with millions of dollars of training and equipment provided by parents Lou and Louanne, the 19-year-old finally claimed the prize he had been dreaming about for almost a few months.

'There was a time in my life when I thought I could just stay at home and spend my parents' money, but they wanted me to go out and actually do something,' said an emotionless Chad Chadle, posting a shot of his Olympic Gold medal beside a stack of $100 bills on the hood of his sports car to Instagram in a bid to increase jealousy among those that he considers to be 'haters'.

'Luckily for me, I was pretty good at a niche, elitist sport, and had the time and the money to pursue my goals. Now that I've scooped an Olympic

> **'Luckily for me, I was pretty good at a niche, elitist sport, and had the time and the money to pursue my goals'**

gold in whatever the fuck you call this country, I'm going to head back to the USA and see if I can sell my inspiring, riches-to-riches story to a movie company or something. Now get the fuck out of my way.'

Chadle's glory has inspired children across America to dream of one day becoming Olympic snowboarders. However, Chadle has described this as 'impossible' as most of them are 'broke as fuck and ugly too'.

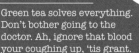

Health and Well-being Tip

Green tea solves everything. Don't bother going to the doctor. Ah, ignore that blood your coughing up, 'tis grant.

FOOTBALL

LOCAL MAN MISSES THE GOOD OLD DAYS OF GAA VIOLENCE

WATERFORD native Packie Herrihan has dismissed the fast-moving, hard-but-fair nature of today's GAA as being 'for snowflakes', and has urged young teams across the country to get back to the leg-breaking, 30-man-brawl days of club football.

Herrihan, who never played football himself, but knows plenty about it, cited Sunday's junior B semi-

final between Kilmahin Gaels and Ballyshacklan as 'proof if proof were needed' that the good old days of matches being 70 per cent footballing skills, 30 per cent jaw-breaking thumps need to return as fast as possible.

Once-hated rivals who would devolve a match into a classic display of disgraceful scenes mere minutes after the first whistle, the Gaels held Ballyshacklan to a 1-09 to 12 points draw without so much as a single yellow card, much to the chagrin of Herrihan, who left with ten minutes to go, cursing loudly in front of everyone in attendance.

'Can you believe I was asked to mind my language because there was children present?' fumed 62-year-old Herrihan, who just really, really wanted to see some young men maim each other today.

'It's ridiculous. What sort of game is it these days? You bring in these black cards and these fair-play ambassadors and this notion that you shouldn't dig the head off the lad that's marking you when you get the ref's back turned. What is the game becoming at all? Maybe some people like all that skillful play, but I preferred it when the team that won was the team that could see the straightest through their concussions.'

Herrihan has vowed to never watch his local team play ever again, but will tune in when the Dublin senior team are playing as 'at least they know how to throw a sly dig or two'.

WITH the increasing importance of social media in terms of driving revenue in sports, WWN has found compelling evidence that suggests Premier League footballers should be allowed to bring their smartphones onto the pitch with them during matches, and tweet about the game as it takes place.

'The amount of people who sit and watch a football match and then act on the advertising that they've seen during that match is falling,' said Denholm Kingston, PR guru and vocal supporter of the Tweeting Footballers Movement.

'So brands are getting less and less return for their investment: this can't last forever. Brands won't keep throwing money at old, dead media. Social media is where it's at. But when the interest in a player is at its peak on any given week, during the games themselves, he's nowhere to be found on Twitter, because he's too busy running around trying to score goals. So our suggestion that players be allowed to post on social media as they play suddenly becomes a whole new, very exciting revenue stream.'

With the actual competitive side of sport being such a small portion of why it gets so much coverage by the media, Kingston's plan to lobby to allow players shill products from the field has gained support, especially from the cash-strapped players who see it as a way of bolstering

SHOULD FOOTBALLERS BE ALLOWED TWEET DURING MATCHES?

their pitiful incomes.

'There's a reason why sport gets so much coverage, why it takes up more space in a newspaper than news about actual nuclear war,' explained Kingston, showing us some mocked-up sample tweets of high-profile players posting selfies while a goal-mouth scramble takes place yards away.

'It's because it makes money. We're not in the business of seeing some kid's childhood dream of scoring in the Premier League come true; we're in the business of slapping as many logos on that kid and getting him in front of as many eyes as we can. If the game he's playing in is watched by two million people, but he himself has five million followers on Twitter, then it only makes sense to allow him to live stream from his phone as the match takes place. And then you throw in the fact that there's 21 other people doing the same thing at the same time... there's really no argument left.'

Concerns that introducing tweeting to the sport would ruin the integrity of the sport have been met with wails of laughter and questions asking, 'What integrity?'

FOOTBALL

LIVERPOOL FAN'S GIRLFRIEND WISHED HE TALKED ABOUT HER LIKE HE DOES MO SALAH

JESSICA Farrelly cut a forlorn figure on the end of her couch yesterday afternoon as she had to contend yet again with the stark reality of her relationship with her boyfriend and Liverpool fan Anthony Coogan, and his undying love for Mohamed Salah.

Farrelly, 27, had been in a happy and romantic union with Coogan, 26, for three years until some time in September 2017, things took a turn for the worse.

'Anthony isn't some monosyllabic knuckle dragger, but yes, it's true to say he doesn't exactly find it easy to

Suburban Dictionary

'Not the full shilling' – the official term in the HSE handbook up until 2013 for describing someone of allegedly reduced mental capacity.

> **'He's turned into fuckin' Shakespeare, spouting sonnets ever since Salah came along'**

express his feelings. Like, it took him two years to say "I love you", and even then he struggled. But he's turned into fuckin' Shakespeare, spouting sonnets ever since Salah came along,' a disgruntled Farrelly explained.

Coogan, now a loose-lipped loved-up lothario when it comes to Salah, has taken to divulging intense proclamations of love any time the star player makes one of his trademark slalom-like darting runs or adds to his already impressive tally of goals this season.

'Just listen to him,' Farrelly sobbed as Coogan committed yet another stirring, heartfelt confession of love to the player Liverpool fans have taken to their heart this season.

'Fucking yes! Get in. Love you, Mo. You beauty,' Coogan giddily expressed as Salah scored against Southampton yesterday, his eyes transfixed on the Egyptian star.

'I don't know what I'd do if he got injured. I couldn't take not having him line out on the pitch and in my heart. Jessica, look, look at him sprint. Jessica! You're not looking, look at him. Look at him, he's so fast! I get goosebumps every time,' Coogan added, piling on the declarations of love for someone he hasn't lived with for the last 18 months.

Farrelly's heartache is only set to continue as Coogan has in recent weeks begun trying to replicate Salah's hairstyle.

MIXED MARTIAL ARTS

28-YEAR-OLD MAN TAKES CONOR MCGREGOR POSTER DOWN FROM WALL

THE bedroom wall of Waterford man Thomas Hickey is looking a little bare today after the father of none made the heavy-hearted decision to end his ebullient and dogged support of former MMA ace Conor McGregor.

It's believed Hickey's decision was motivated by his dissatisfaction with the former UFC champ's behaviour this last week, which saw him cause criminal damage resulting in injuries, or as people who still have McGregor's posters on their walls called it, 'a highly staged promotion for an upcoming fight, so fucking relax.'

The poster which depicted McGregor fighting was held up on Hickey's wall using Blu-Tack, but with a simple tug at the corners, McGregor's dominance over the sales executive's wall had come to an end.

'I'm not going to stand here and lie to you. That wasn't easy. I'm upset. He used to be my hero, someone I looked up to as a fellow man in my late 20s,' Hickey told WWN Sport, tears forming in his eyes.

'I can only defend the man's exceptional talents for so long while he's engaging in harmless hijinks, such as using homophobic language, allegedly assaulting people, speeding, and throwing stuff through bus windows.'

Alluding to yet more allegations of allegedly doing other alleged stuff that has been alleged of McGregor, Hickey said his desire and appetite for following the fighting fortunes of the Dubliner has formally come to an end.

'Younger lads than me might not remember, but that McGregor chap was an MMA fighter before he was a lad who turned up in memes and viral videos, but I don't think that Conor is coming back,' Hickey said, before falling to his knees and breaking down in floods of tears.

HUNGOVER LOCAL STRIKER SUPRISED AS ANYONE HE SCORED A HAT-TRICK

LIAM Grotty, striker for local Waterford Sunday league team Rovers Celtic United, admitted to being as surprised as anyone that necking an unconfirmed number of pints Saturday night had no negative effect on his performance against Dunmore Celtic.

The striker, described privately by teammates as 'piss poor', bagged himself a hat-trick to generous applause from the seven spectators, which included two dogs, but admits to being hungover to such an extent that he has little memory of the 84 minutes he played before being substituted.

'My third was a header, was it? Here boi, have you any Lucozade? I'm in bits,' confirmed the striker who rolled back the years to net his first hat-trick in over 10 years. However, it is the 15th time this season he has played with a hangover.

The goals from Grotty came during the brief spells in the game when he wasn't heaving with his hands on his knees, wishing he hadn't ordered those shots.

'We had a delay to kick off which didn't help,' Rovers Celtic United player-manager, 46-year-old Tommy Deelings, told WWN Sport. 'The pitch had to be lined and then we had to remove some vomit from the pitch which Liamo put there during the warm up. But we're happy with his performance. We're thinking of keeping him on the drink. The opposition were no match for our fairly average standard of football.'

FOOTBALL

MO SALAH ASCENDS TO HEAVEN

LIVERPOOL and Egyptian forward Mo Salah ascended to Heaven/Jannah directly after being substituted last night, with God deeming him too precious an example of celestial perfection to risk keeping down on Earth any longer.

A thunderous sound pulsed through Anfield following Salah's two goals and two assists, with a shaft of immense light striking down on the forward as Liverpool fans wept, at first with sorrow, before becoming over-awed with pure unadulterated love.

Did You Know?

St Patrick also drove unreasonably high car insurance out of Ireland? However, it has since returned, more powerful than ever.

'Behold, your Saviour ascends,' a booming voice said, beckoning to the diminutive figure of Salah as he rose skywards, with the forward himself looking on in wonder and disbelief as he travelled on his way to meet the one true common God who watches over all of humanity.

While initially thought to be taken to the ceaseless paradise of the afterlife, some sources close to the eternal kingdom suggest God was in need of a star player for his annual inter-galactic cross-universe football derby between the Zeebnonian galaxy and the nefarious galactic tyrant Kerkranus.

'Even in other universes, which adhere to different types of gravity, Mo's pace will be unstoppable and his calmness in front of the goal will come in handy against the Zeebnonian's

> **'Even in other universes, which adhere to different types of gravity, Mo's pace will be unstoppable'**

30-foot tall, 14-handed, three-headed keeper,' a heavenly source explained.

There was a brief delay in Salah's ascension as the merciful creator of the universe, in an act of kindness, paused momentarily to bring the Roma team back to life for the final ten minutes of the Champions League semi-final first leg after they were completely obliterated by an unstoppable Liverpool side.

fc-angusht.ru
FC-Angusht
vk.com/fcangusht93
fc_angusht_official

RUSSIA TRIALS BEAR REFEREES FOR UPCOMING WORLD CUP

AFTER a recent spate of unsavoury incidents involving the intimidation of referees, Russia has proposed an innovative solution to the cancer on football that is professional footballers.

Famed for constantly diving to win penalties, cheating to gain minor advantages throughout each second of a game, and having shit haircuts, footballers are potentially the only element of the upcoming World Cup that could possibly ruin it for fans.

However, Russia, fresh from annexing Crimea, interfering in international elections, poisoning people on English soil, and aiding and abetting the murderous Assad regime, may have the solution all football fans can get behind: bear referees.

After successfully trialling a bear as an official ball carrier at a recent Russian third division match, Russian World Cup officials have confirmed they will go ahead with plans to allow bear referees officiate all games at the 2018 World Cup.

'Anyone try to do like Buffon, referee bear will do to player like Leonardo DiCaprio in film *Revenant*,' explained bear tamer and head of refereeing at the upcoming World Cup some people are somehow still looking forward to, Igor Siminov.

Initial training has shown bears seem to have a better grasp of VAR than human referees.

Many people meanwhile have decried the use of an innocent animal in such a way, stating that the presence of bears in any capacity at the World Cup would lead to them boycotting the tournament.

'Really? All those North Korean workers killed building our stadiums and you care more about bear? Good, this shows you have respect for bear, makes him perfect for refereeing,' Siminov confirmed before cruelly yanking on a chain attached to the neck of a North Korean slave.

FIFA CONFIRMS EXPANSION OF WORLD CUP TO 48 TEAMS 'BECAUSE MONEY'

FIFA President Gianni Infantino has confirmed that the footballing world has been gifted a utopian 48-team World Cup tournament that will restore the wide-eyed optimism and joy to the game that it has sorely been lacking.

Infantino, dressed head to toe in a gold-plated suit, when asked why FIFA delegates had made the unanimous decision to vote in favour of expanding the tournament from 32 teams to 48, spoke with the childlike passion for the game so many people around the world love.

'We're going to make, how do you say, a fucking fortune,' Infantino expressed, putting the fears of fans, who had for some time suspected the move was a flagrant bid to simply earn more money, to rest.

Plans are already in place to secure more sponsors for the 2026 World Cup, and negotiations for the TV rights are underway. However, safeguarding the future of the game and funding grassroots remain the priorities.

'We could make €500 million more than we make out of the tournament now. I wish we expanded to 188 teams to be honest, think of what I could charge to the expenses account then,' Infantino shared, stressing that integrity and selfless governance of the game came before any consideration of money.

'By expanding to 48 teams, I keep the smaller countries happy and that means I won't have my leadership challenged and I can stay on this gold-encrusted gravy train,' Infantino added.

FIFA also announced the creation of a new online bribery submission system for those countries wishing to bid for the 2026 World Cup.

RTÉ CANCELS WORLD CUP COVERAGE, DECIDES TO SHOW ITALIA '90 ON REPEAT

In a bid to soften the blow of Ireland not qualifying for the 2018 World Cup in Russia, RTÉ has taken the unprecedented step of binning their exclusive and costly World Cup coverage in favour of just showing Italia '90 on repeat.

RTÉ viewers will be given the chance to marvel at Ireland's legendary quarter-final starring turn at Italia '90, in what many unbiased Irish fans call the greatest of all World Cups. The rerun will extend to all aspects of Irish life, with Crazy Prices, the Punt, old Tayto packets and a Fianna Fáil government set to reappear as well.

Packie's penalty heroics. O'Leary's game-winning peno strike. RTÉ is allowing everyone the chance to forget that Ireland is not in this year's World Cup. The broadcaster will give the public an option to choose a special version of the Italy game which cuts off and goes to the old 'technical difficulties' page just as Totò Schillaci bears down on goal.

'We know some audiences might want to see Messi, Salah, Ronaldo and the rest battle it out, but we're going to show Ireland v Romania maybe 10 or 12 times while the 2018 tournament is going on instead,' explained one RTÉ spokesperson who surprisingly has received no emails or letters of complaint. In fact, so welcomed is the decision, RTÉ received its first ever letter of praise from the public.

In a bid to further cast memories back to happier times when Ireland could qualify for World Cups, World Cup anthem 'Put 'Em Under Pressure' will be placed back on top of the pop charts and played routinely in nightclubs around the 1 a.m. mark. This Italia '90 repeat will culminate in an open-top bus parade down O'Connell Street with some sound employers giving their employees the day off to recover from the celebrations.

LOCAL 'INTELLECTUAL' HASN'T WATCHED A SINGLE SECOND OF THE WORLD CUP

A local Dublin man who has revealed he is above trivial pursuits such as acknowledging the existence of the football World Cup is, according to experts, some kind of once-in-a-generation intellectual behemoth.

Cormac Cranny has informed everyone he has come into contact with in recent weeks that he either 'didn't know there was a World Cup on', 'hasn't watched a second of the football' or 'ha, no, think I'm a bit beyond watching idiots chase a ball', sparking speculation that he might have a sharper mind than Stephen Hawking, Immanuel Kant, Bertrand Russell or Albert Einstein at the peak of their intellectual powers.

'I keep getting asked who do you think will win the cup or whatever it is those people are playing for, but honestly, I'm just not into football. I prefer doing something meaningful with my spare time, thank you very much,' Cranny explained, even though he's glued to his phone watching shite like the rest of us.

The systems analyst was able to confirm that football is a maelstrom of pathetically performative macho nonsense and helpfully implied that women have no interest it and that it just isn't credible to imply people could like football and also have other diverse interests and hobbies.

Cranny's pursuits are presumably a little too sophisticated for simple football-watching folk, and likely include nestling his nostril in glasses of red wine and breathing in sharply while watching movies with subtitles, something football yobs would know nothing about.

'Who needs football when you have literature and poetry,' confirmed the 26-year-old who last read a book when he was in college and doesn't even need those fucking glasses.

WATCH OUT!

WHAT TO DO IN THE EVENT OF ENGLAND WINNING THE WORLD CUP

LAST night, the England team did the unthinkable; they progressed through to the next round of the competition by beating a team in a penalty shoot-out. As such, we have moved the England World Cup Doomsday Clock forward by five minutes to 11.55 p.m., the closest it has been in decades to 12 midnight and total England World Cup victory.

Although the chances of England winning the World Cup remain a distant and improbable threat, it would be foolish to not prepare for such an unthinkable scenario. As recent events have shown, this current England squad do not care for people who just want to see them crash out in the knockout stages so that we can all have something to laugh at. Unrest continues to grow in many countries as to what would happen if football does indeed come home, and, as such, we have compiled a survival guide for those caught up in the horror of an English World Cup victory:

1) Do not look at the flash
Should Southgate's men break through the defences put in place to stop them and actually achieve World Cup glory, you will see a bright flash followed by a deafening roar. The flash is caused by millions of English people throwing their arms up in the air at once, causing their jerseys to lift over their white pot bellies, simultaneously reflecting the sunlight and blinding anyone within 5,000 miles. Do not look directly into the flash. Shield your eyes, and hold your nose to avoid being overcome by the ensuing stench of body odour, Lynx Africa, and spilled Carling.

2) Stop, drop, anguish
After England win the World Cup, stop, drop, and wail in anguish. Continue rocking over and back on the ground for as long as you want. The safest place to be is under a table, or under a sturdy doorjamb. Keep repeating, 'Fuck sake, they'll be fucking impossible now', over and over again.

3) Identify England sympathisers
Pro-England sentiment in your country may be stronger than you think. Listen out for traitors who say, 'Ah it's nice for them all the same' or 'I'm happy for Southgate'. These people may simply be trying to survive by cosying up to the English by any means necessary, or they may actually be glad that England has won. Either way, they need a kick in the bollocks.

4) Prepare yourself for a World Cup winter
The resulting fallout of an England World Cup victory will last a minimum of four years, where there is a chance of beating them at the next tournament. This time will be arduous, and, like, super annoying. Scientists believe that the smugness from an England World Cup victory may actually cause crops to die in the ground, the sky to darken and the sun to be blotted out. Should England win, there is nothing we can do to prevent this. All we can do is pray it never happens.

5) Oh yeah, take your iodine tablets
They can't hurt.

HARDCORE GAA FAN BLINDS HIMSELF TO AVOID SEEING ANY OF THE WORLD CUP

ABSOLUTELY livid that the game beloved by the vile British empire and used by the occupying British forces decade after decade to stamp out any indigenous Irish culture is still on the TV all day, every day, one hardcore GAA fan has blinded himself in a bid to ensure his eyes aren't blemished by the sight of foreign games on Irish TV.

The pathetic game played by wimpy millionaires who just dive about the place is one so hated by Mayo man Dermot O'Doland that he took his own sight to avoid being exposed to its evil, no matter the cost.

'It poisons Irish people. Like, have you no national pride, no love of Ireland? No, of course not, you do be off watching soccer, taking the Queen's shilling,' O'Doland said to his housemates as they took in some of the action in Russia, forcing O'Doland to take drastic action.

Mixing together several household cleaning items kept under the sink, O'Doland doused his eyes with them in an effort to keep his GAA proud eyes from being sullied by the filth of soccer, used as a tool in the British empire's long history of violence and oppression across the globe.

O'Doland came to regret the decision, in between violent screams of pain, when his friends let out shouts of complaint, giving out about one particularly awful dive in a World Cup match.

'Describe the dive to me in detail, this is why I'd never let my kids play any of this shite,' O'Doland said, visibly erect at the thought of someone diving in a game of soccer.

VAR REPLAY CONFIRMS WOMEN IN CROWD AT WORLD CUP ARE ATTRACTIVE

FOOTBALL fans fearing the advent of video assistant referees (VAR) in World Cup matches would ruin games have been given yet another example of how slick and unobtrusive the technology can be, with games flowing at the same pace despite the need to consult replays of controversial incidents.

The absorbing contest last night between Russia and Egypt saw match officials rely on VAR throughout the game, as it appeared the referee, cameraman or director of the live TV feed needed help in confirming if attractive women do indeed attend the World Cup.

Some fans confessed to be confused as to why their TV continuously cut to a shot of one objectively attractive woman in the

crowd, but with last night's Russian game FIFA officials provided confirmation that VAR was investigating whether or not totally hot female women babes are in the crowd.

'Look, VAR is there to help the referee make decisions or become more aware of incidents on the pitch, and obviously the only explanation for why some 15 or so minutes of each game is spent cutting to women in the crowd is not blatant and lazy sexism, but a technical refereeing operation,' one FIFA spokesman confirmed.

Despite the abundance of VAR replays proving that attractive women are fans of football and supporting their respective countries at the most high-profile sports tournament in the world, FIFA stresses that this must be rechecked after every available opportunity.

'We can't just presume there are hot women in the crowd; we've got to use VAR replays to ensure that is the case. We'd ask fans to please be patient with VAR and the officials using it with the help of the TV channel. It will be necessary at times to slow down the replay when women in the crowd are jumping up and down,' the spokesman confirmed.

FOOTBALL

PROFESSIONAL SPORTSMAN THANKS GOD FOR ALLOWING HIM TO SCORE GOAL

DESPITE routinely training with an unrelenting determination for the majority of his every waking day since the age of four, one leading sports star has chosen to give all the credit to God after the athlete landed the game-winning goal for the football team he represents.

'Without God, none of this is possible. I thank God for the ability to do all this. Praise Jesus'

Seemingly unwilling to acknowledge the part his own dedication played in his development into an elite sportsperson, Jayvon Devine sought to single out The Almighty and give Him the credit for carrying out a sporting performance Devine himself conducted.

'Without God, none of this is possible. I thank God for the ability to do all this. Praise Jesus,' Devine explained, simplifying his 20-year-long effort to perfect his football skill sets, day in, day out, as he sacrificed enjoying a normal life enjoyed by his non-football playing peers.

A closer study of Devine's post-game interviews reveal he singles out God for praise when it comes to his football skills, but is more ready to accept praise for dressing himself in the morning, driving from A to B and being able to push doors when they are clearly marked 'PUSH' rather than mistakenly pulling on them.

God, in response, blushing from embarrassment, remarked, 'You're welcome', when asked for comment by WWN Sport.

FOOTBALL

WORK 5-A-SIDE TEAM MAKE RECORD BID FOR POLISH LAD FROM WAREHOUSE

THE fortunes of the 5-a-side team from McCrahhan's Builders Providers outside Waterford City may be about to take a turn for the better, as negotiations to sign the young Polish chap who drives one of the forklifts in the yard enter their final phase.

The 24-year-old, really tall and very fit-looking Polish chap, whose name is unknown, but the rest of the yard staff call him Mick, has agreed to come to the local Astro on Friday to fill in for one of the floor staff who has a wedding that day, providing he can be finished up at 9 p.m. to go do a shift on the door of a pub in town.

Player-manager Seamie Dooley has expressed his delight at the progress being made, and is looking forward to the match this Friday against 'those pricks from the car lot across the road'.

'The team from Lennon's Volkswagen have been creaming us out of it for the past year, but with that useless prick Darren from the floor out and this big Polish lad from the yard in, we have an advantage,' said Dooley, checking his 5-a-side WhatsApp group to make sure that he has numbers for Friday.

'Mick, or whatever his real name is, will be a valuable asset for us when it comes to blasting the ball from 40 yards out and pretending that he didn't know that was against the rules because he speaks fuck all English. We'll fucking trounce them.'

Dooley went on to add that Mick also looks like he'd be alright 'in nets' if the need arises.

GAA COACH RECRUITING STOCKY 7-YEAR-OLDS OVER 6 FOOT TALL

A LOCAL GAA coach has announced a fresh recruitment drive for the under-7s football team he coaches, stressing, however, that he is only in the market for broad-shouldered children who are 6 foot and over, WWN Sport can reveal.

With the ever-increasing physicality of football, and the attritional and abrasive tactics employed during games, it has never been more important for coaches to ignore skill and technique in favour of massive lads who could throw you through a wall.

'Here at Ballyhibberty Gaels, we're just looking to get the young fellas enjoying a pressure-free atmosphere where they can learn a few skills and just enjoy playing football with friends,' explained local coach Eoin Bovaney.

'The last thing we want at our club, which is the heartbeat of the community, is for parents screaming at kids, or kids just standing on the sideline for the whole season not getting any minutes on the field. They're only babies at the end of the day,' added Bovaney, striking a refreshing tone for a coach.

'Having said that, I don't want any of these little pricks turning up if they can't bench press 100 kgs or have never been asked, "How's the weather up there?" We need seven-year-olds built like fucking tanks, ready for battle.'

The fresh appeal for players over six foot is only the beginning for Ballyhibberty Gaels under-7s as new recruits will enter a new training camp which sees them lashing the protein powder into themselves and flipping over tires wherever they go.

NORTH KOREAN PROPOSAL TO OPEN WINTER GAMES WITH NUCLEAR EXPLOSION REJECTED

A PROPOSAL by North Korea to detonate a 40 kiloton nuclear bomb to celebrate the opening of the Winter Games has been rejected by neighbours South Korea, WWN has learned.

Officials for supreme leader Kim Jong-un travelled to Seoul on Monday for their first high-level talks in more than two years, ending with an agreement to allow athletes from the hermit kingdom to participate in the event.

However, a proposal to 'light up the sky' with a nuclear blast was deemed 'unnecessary' by Winter Games organisers, instead insisting on a normal, but substantial, fireworks display for the opening ceremony.

'We appreciate the sentiment, but feel that detonating an atomic bomb like that may not be in good taste, considering the world's current climate,' Chun Hae-sung, South Korean Vice Unification Minister, said after the morning talks. 'Obviously we have to think of the effects of such a blast on the environment too, but it's a nice gesture all the same, and I'm sure Kim meant well.'

Despite a promise by North Korea to keep the blast radius on their side of the border, and 'over some farms they no longer use', the South Korean minister remained adamant in his decision, but did agree to a compromise, which will allow Kim Jong-un to personally win several events, including figure skating, curling and ski-jumping, without actually taking part in them.

'It's not ideal, but he did put the hand out first,' concluded the minister.

Suburban Dictionary

'You absolute Dáil' – someone who does nothing, but tries telling everyone they're doing a lot of hard work.

WEB NEWS

SEXTON'S DROP GOAL UPLOADED TO PORNHUB

DUE to the fact its erotic content has a 100 per cent success rate in inducing disturbing groans of pleasure, Jonathan Sexton's last-gasp drop goal against France has been uploaded successfully to online pornography site, Pornhub.

While experts had previously believed it was impossible to be sexually attracted to and aroused by a piece of rugby, Irish users have proven such assumptions to be incorrect as a video of the drop kick has been viewed 62 million times already with multiple uploads of the video accounting for .00000096 per cent of Pornhub's entire traffic yesterday.

'It's right up there with "Backdoor Milf Action 5" and the *Father Ted* parody porn stuff as Ireland's most beloved over 18s, sexually explicit viewing material,' one Pornhub spokesperson shared with WWN.

There have been reports that many men find themselves breathing heavily and becoming increasingly excited while watching the video, before retiring into a lengthy refractory period, exhausted.

'Obviously they have trouble lasting the 41 phases, but the final five or six

'It's right up there with "Backdoor Milf Action 5" and the *Father Ted* parody porn stuff as Ireland's most beloved over 18s, sexually explicit viewing material'

seconds leading up to the drop goal seems the ideal length of time for most to get their own "kicks",' added the Pornhub spokesperson, who crunched the numbers and hard data.

'The majority of women, however, enjoy the entire 41 phases before collapsing in a satisfied heap.' Despite claims to the contrary, the average man only lasts up to four phases.

Historically, crime levels are often seen decreasing during sporting events such as soccer matches; however, analysts saw a different trend during Ireland's first match of the Six Nations tournament.

'There was a dramatic decrease in the number of people ordering

Chapter Six:

Having successfully spent the months from February to October working undercover as a Spanish student in Dublin, it is finally time for me to return to my handlers at the Ministerio de Fomento to relay my findings on the Irish public transport system, and how they may be used to improve the Spanish bus and rail services. I will tell them that a public transport system functions best when it functions at all, and that anyone living in a city centre should prepare for the worst every time they leave to go to work. Maybe their bus will show up; maybe it won't. Maybe their train will arrive on time; maybe their train will arrive half an hour late, because what organisation could be expected to keep track of five separate lines operating at the same time? I will tell them that no security is needed on trains or buses because sometimes, anti-social violence is 'just a bit of craic', and I will tell them to make sure and pay everyone the same amount of money, because it only takes one person unhappy with their wages to grind an entire network to a screeching halt at the drop of a hat, holding thousands of commuters hostage until their pay demands are met. And I will tell them all this, with a very hoarse voice. Ten months later, and I have no idea why we Spanish students must insist on yelling all the fucking time.

soy lattes in Starbucks and asking to speak to the manager. There were zero instances of Audis and BMWs being parked on double yellow lines and, most intriguingly, disabled car parking spaces outside yacht clubs were empty and available for use by disabled people,' one analyst explained.

The NSFW clip is best viewed in a quiet room by yourself, which allows you all the alone time you need.

FOOTBALL

HAND OF FROG: A LOOK BACK AT THE GREATEST INJUSTICE IN HUMAN HISTORY

WAR! Genocide! Famine! Some more war again! Few, if any events in human history can rival the anguish and devastation wrought by the destructive handball carried out by French war criminal Thierry Henry; war, famine and genocide are indeed three of the things that simply pale in comparison.

It was like a bomb went off, only much worse than an actual bomb and Ireland, a nation full of once-proud people, has never fully recovered from the events of 18 November 2009.

WWN looks back on the night the entire world was changed forever as one of France's finest footballers committed an act *Time* magazine would go on to call 'that rare travesty that dwarfs the crimes and inhumanity of the Holocaust.'

Of course, everyone has vivid memories of that night and the events that followed. Who could forget that enduring image of the French Embassy in Dublin set on fire and ransacked by Irish supporters drunk on grief? But there are lesser stories to tell too, the smaller details which give life to a tragedy never fully dealt with and processed by those innocent people altered by the Hand of Frog.

'I still vomit at the sight of baguettes,' shares Dublin accountant Damien O'Brien, who was one of the 79,145 sets of eyes in the Stade de France who clearly saw what the referee Martin Hansson failed to spot. Hansson, now an honorary French citizen, received scorn for his performance, but the fault lies with FIFA who should never have allowed a blind man to referee a game.

'I was standing directly behind a great big beam obscuring my view in the top tier in the last row, but I saw it clearly and I wasn't the only one to hear Thierry say, "Watch this, I will now appal with a handball. I shut you up, as we go to the World Cup." That's how evil and twisted a mind that maniac has, he had the cold-hearted presence of mind to write a shite poem about what he was doing mid-handball. It's as bizarre as it is disgusting,' O'Brien added of the moment, in an account that WWN can personally verify as true.

Amidst the hysteria, many people say they saw a second hand that didn't belong to Henry pat the ball across the goal and into the path of William Gallas; the 'second handballer on the pitch' conspiracy theory continues to have its fans to this day. We will have to wait until 2059, the 50th anniversary of the handball for the documents relating to the incident to be declassified by FIFA.

Shortly after the final whistle, a diplomatic crisis had begun. Then President of Ireland, Mary McAleese,

in attendance at the game, headbutted Nicolas Sarkozy before returning to Dublin.

In a move very similar to America renaming French fries 'freedom fries' during the Iraq War, the Irish government banned thin and creepy moustaches as well as snooty laughter that sounded particularly French. Laughter that sort of sounds like 'uh haw haw haaaw' is still banned in Ireland today.

But what of the man at the centre of the incident? Henry delighted in his country's progress to the World Cup, and signed lucrative endorsement deals as big brands clamoured to be associated with his cheating hand. Chanel released a line of Henry gloves, the Eiffel Tower was replaced by a giant hand, particularly odd and wealthy French people got surgery on their hands so they looked exactly like Henry's. The France and Barcelona Arsenal star would later regret these endorsements and claimed his hand 'acted alone', but he fooled no one.

The FAI, those noble protectors of Irish football, called for 100 days of mourning and in a move criticised by the few Irish people who simply said 'move on', they erased all records of the fact that even if the handball hadn't happened Ireland would still merely have taken France to extra time in the play-off.

The head of the FAI, patriot John Delaney, went on hunger strike outside FIFA headquarters for 89 days, demanding justice for Ireland in the form of a highly questionable one-off lump-sum payment of €5 million that no one needed to be made aware of.

Amazingly, the French government has still never officially apologised for the Hand of Frog, and despite an arrest warrant being issued by Irish police, Henry remains at large. It will never be known whether or not Ireland would have beaten Spain 17-0 in the final of the World Cup in South Africa.

Ireland continues to mourn, with a week's long silence observed every year starting on 18 November. It is hoped an upcoming film, *Hand of Frog*, starring Daniel Day-Lewis as the football, will help the nation heal.

SYRIA

ADORABLE LETTER EIGHT-YEAR-OLD WROTE TO THERESA MAY AND DONALD TRUMP FOLLOWING SYRIAN STRIKES

THE world *needs* to see the adorable letters an eight-year-old girl wrote to Theresa May and Donald Trump after the recent Syrian airstrikes.

Amy Williams, a second-class pupil in St Stephen's Primary in Waterford, penned an absolutely heartwarming and inspirational pair of letters to the two world leaders following the 14 April airstrikes on Syria. Although she's only eight, her words are very important and moving. Amy's letters is GOALS.

Dear Theresa May,
I think you need to cop the fuck on to yourself and act in your country's best interests instead of being a horrible cantankerous bitch looking to make her place in the history books. Just remember, nothing can hide that decrepit soul of yours from seeping through your grey, mothball smelling exterior, so don't try and pull the wool over my 8 year old eyes. I see through your bullshit. I bet you drown puppies every morning, you despicable piece of cockroach shit. Please, stop selling weapons to your scumbag, woman beating Saudi peers, you shameful bag of puss.
Thanks,
Amy, 8

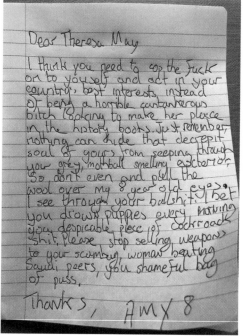

What a dote! That's some serious shade she's throwing at Theresa May, but not in a 'women tearing each other down' kind of way. Theresa May really should pay attention. Preach Amy, PREACH! Amy then went on to address the US President with an equally cute approach:

Dear Donald Trump,
Instead of bombing countries you have no clue about, how about fixing America's problems instead of sticking your fat fucking orange nose into everyone else's business? You psychopathic fucktards spend $600 billion every year on the military,

'Instead of bombing countries you have no clue about, how about fixing America's problems instead of sticking your fat fucking orange nose into everyone else's business?'

yet still can't win a fucking war or manage to function normally as a society. And then, when the poor people you've bombed retaliate, you instruct the news to call them terrorists? You and all those people pulling your strings ARE the fucking terrorists. The world doesn't belong to America; it belongs to all 7 billion of us, you perverted inbred slimy bastard of a man.
Kind regards,
Amy, 8

It touches the heart when a young person makes such valid statements like these to world leaders. Who's cutting onions in here? No, we're not crying, you're crying. Good to know that we are in safe hands for the future. Amy is straight up killin' it today. Giving out serious inspiration. Thanks for the free content Aims!

Wonderful World of Science

Safety authorities had to shut down a TCD lab earlier this year when it was discovered they were experimenting with putting in more MiWadi and less water.

DRUGS

NEIGHBOURS smoking cannabis in their own home is one of the country's biggest problems right now and causes a range of social issues, including homelessness, poor-quality health care, low minimum wage and the housing crisis, and encourages corruption in state-run entities. So what action can you take?

Luckily we have put together this unique article you won't find anywhere else which has not been in any way sponsored by anyone with an agenda against cannabis.

Is it legal for people to smoke cannabis in their own home?

Absolutely not. No matter if you own your home or rent it, you're not allowed avail of this naturally occurring plant that has proven health benefits because the government and its pharmaceutical partners don't get any revenue from it – revenue they can later avoid paying little or no tax on. Personal decisions on what you do with your body, and what you put into it, were made illegal years ago in Ireland for your own good as you are incapable of making your own decisions. Just obey this rule and you won't be put in jail longer than a child rapist. Good citizen.

If I call the gardaí, will my neighbours find out it was me who ratted them out?

Of course not. An Garda Síochána is a tight-knit institution devoid of any corruption or malice and has a glowing reputation when it comes to keeping their mouth shut... when needed. The gardaí are the most sophisticated police force in Ireland, unrivalled in their field. Your pothead neighbours will just think it's all down to bad luck that their home got raided, just as they were putting their kids to bed ahead of school the next day. You go right ahead there and make that call, you champion of the people, you. Rat those bastards out.

What will happen to my neighbours if the gardaí are informed?

Who cares? They're criminals! Think about all the damage they're doing if

WHAT CAN I DO IF MY NEIGHBOURS ARE SMOKING CANNABIS?

you don't call the guards: generating revenue for weird YouTube videos about ancient aliens, playing FIFA 17 throughout the night, eating tonnes and tonnes of sugary and savoury snacks. You're doing them a favour by ratting them out. With a bit of luck they'll be all over the courts section of the local newspapers next week for the whole neighbourhood to see. And if they're renting, hopefully lose their home, job, and have their kids taken off them and sent to one of Ireland's flawless foster

care homes. Sentences for offenders can be anything up to 10 years in prison, or five times the sentence for white-collar crimes in Ireland.

NOTE: it is illegal to rat out wealthy neighbours who may be involved in politics, finance or the judicial system, so check social status first.

In tomorrow's edition: Soundproofing Your Home From Your Abusive Alcoholic Neighbours

EXCLUSIVE

FIVE DECISIONS MORE REGRETTABLE THAN YOUR CHERYL TWEEDY HAND TATTOO

IT has been almost seven years since you opted to deface the side of your hand with a traditional Polynesian Maori-style tattoo that you copied from your idol, Cheryl Tweedy. But don't lament over past mistakes, we've found five more regrettable decisions to take your mind off of that permanent blobby blue mess on your hand you once called art.

5) Marrying local man Leslie Cole
Your decision to marry local 7-a-side striker Leslie Cole in 2006 was probably one of your most regrettable decisions to date, mainly because you didn't really know the man from Adam, apart from being the only black man in the parish that could play football whose second name was Cole. Bribing him with €25,000 into marrying you was a terrible idea, but paying him a further €10,000 to cheat on you some four years later was just damn stupid. However, your divorce did make the courts section of your local newspaper, so there's that, we suppose.

4) Becoming a judge in X-Factor Carrick-On-Suir
Now, we're not saying you did a terrible job, but hiring a bus for 48 people to bring them from Mulligan's Tavern to your council house in Mooncoin at 2 a.m. for 'the judges' houses segment' was actually insane. To top it off, your incessant crying during the whole bit was disturbing, especially when you decided at 7 a.m. not to bring any of your singers through to the next round as 'they weren't good enough' – no wonder the pub owner never asked you back the following year.

3) Marrying cafe owner John Tobin under the condition he would change his name by deed poll to Fernandez-Versini
Yeah, so, this was actually an awful decision, considering John later joined the priesthood and vowed never to look at another woman again. Fr John actually loved you, despite the short three-month courtship and then subsequent divorce 'for no reason'. You're actually a terrible person. We have no words for this.

2) Grooming a local 18-year-old busker and getting pregnant
Look, we know turning 40 can be tough for a twice-divorced woman with an awful culchie accent, but praying on naive young male musicians on the street for two years before securing your 'Liam' is actually criminal. Although William Penn may be a fine young man and doting father of your son, Bear, he is 20 years your junior and has no idea about your lifelong fascination with Cheryl Tweedy, until of course the next time she splits with her partner.

1) That full buttock tattoo
Actually, at this stage in your life, covering that area of your body in a full rose tattoo isn't a bad thing. However, wearing your pyjama bottoms in Tesco with the cheeks of your arse hanging out isn't cool. No one wants to see that kind of thing. Especially when you paid a local alcoholic six cans of Tuborg to imprint the design, using only a compass and the ink from several blue biros.

The Solution Zone!
Noting the dire state the world is in today, WWN proposes practical solutions to some of Ireland's and the world's most pressing issues.

Ireland's Health Service:
– WWN suggests the novel idea of hiring someone to run the health service properly.

– There is always a chronic shortage of beds in hospitals, but if we made every bed a double bed, sickly patients could share with one another. If the budget doesn't allow for this, sleeping 'tops and tails' would be fine.

– The health service is plagued by the fact ungrateful Irish nurses and doctors leave the country as soon as they qualify. We propose imposing a ban on these work-shy ingrates leaving Ireland and then forcing them into working long shifts for less pay than they would get abroad. No, it's not slavery, it's a 'mandatory patriotic work' order.

– A free health service only works if people who are really sick get treated. Introducing 'time-wasting' fines for people who turn up to A&E departments already passed the point of no return. That's just selfish; they could be taking the place in the queue ahead of someone genuinely important, like the relative of a local TD.

– Roll out more GPs for patients to avail of. This stuff is beyond obvious. GPs, or as they are otherwise known 'Google Practitioners', are trained professionals who can help the public. Simply tell a GP your symptoms, let them Google it and tell them you're having a heart-attack cancer stroke and stop bloody wasting the HSE's time.

AVIATION

WE TAKE A TRIP ON 'AIR FORCE A HAON'

WHEN Michael D. Higgins travels, he travels in style. Flanked by two of the Irish Air Force's most elite Spitfire pilots, 'Air Force A Haon' carries our country's premier to crucial engagements all around the world, and WWN have become the first newspaper to have an exclusive trip on the luxury aircraft.

Joining Michael D. Higgins on his daily jaunt to Galway for a poetry reading, WWN boarded the specially modified single-engine Cessna on the lawn out the back of Áras An Uachtaráin, before taking our seat in the passenger hutch located in the rear of the cabin. Michael D. soon joined us, got up on his booster seat so that he could see out the window, and we were off, scraping the bottom of the fuselage on the papal cross as we circled out of Dublin.

Roaring as loud as we could to be heard over the drone of the 2 L diesel engine, we quizzed Michael D. on his travel traditions, but unfortunately we were unable to hear anything he

> **'It will attempt to make the transatlantic crossing to America for the St Patrick's Day celebrations'**

said back to us. The president then fell asleep and didn't wake up until we landed in Galway.

There were concerns when the co-pilot blessed himself and flung himself out of the aircraft with no parachute over Mullingar, but a quick rosary from the on-board cleric was enough to miraculously solve the blaring klaxon and red-flashing beacon that had alarmed the Air Force member to fling himself to his doom.

Onboard snacks consisted of a bag of Tayto and a purple Snack, and we were treated to an episode of *Father Ted* with the subtitles on, played on an iPad that ran out of battery seven minutes outside Dublin.

The landing at Galway was a perfect success, if success is measured by bare survival.

The aircraft was then put on the back of a lorry and driven back to Dublin, with the president explaining to us that the plane can only fly 'with the wind, never against it'.

'Air Force A Haon' will be put into storage until March, when it will attempt to make the transatlantic crossing to America for the St Patrick's Day celebrations, hopefully avoiding the tragic fate of the previous 'Air Force A Haon', which crashed down somewhere outside Iceland in 1971, resulting in the first death of the then-president Éamon de Valera.

Suburban Dictionary

'Wee scissors' – ideally suited for trimming nails, nose hairs. Although easily lost, only one pair is allowed in any given household.

EXCLUSIVE

HOW TO HEAR WHAT PEOPLE SAY ABOUT YOU AFTER YOU LEAVE A ROOM

DO you ever wonder what your friends, family or co-workers say about you after you leave the room? Perhaps they compliment you, perhaps they let slip some closely held disdain for you. Either way, it's bound to be fascinating, and a key insight into how the world sees you.

WWN has some more subtle ways to find out these details, rather than simply camping up outside the door with our ear pressed to the wood, listening intently for any mention of your name. Here's how you can eavesdrop subtly and learn more about yourself!

1) Have an excuse

All you really have to do is have some reason to stay at the door after you leave such as tying your shoelace, checking your phone, anything except just standing there. If someone rounds the corner and sees you checking your phone, they won't think anything of it. If someone opens the door unexpectedly and finds you there just pressed against it, they're going to know you were snooping. Have some activity to cover yourself!

2) Listen intently for a minute, at most

If people are going to say anything about you, they'll say it in the moments after you leave, before moving on to whatever business they're getting down to. So you only need to listen for a minute to see if they're talking about you or not.

3) Wait, hang on

Did someone just say, 'Bring out the gimp?'… what the fuck?

4) Oh no

Holy shit, they're all fucking each other! Your whole family/circle of friends/upper management team! It's a hideously depraved orgy, which by the sounds of things is taking place without any form of lubrication whatsoever. You cannot see what is going on, but the screams alone paint a vivid, sordid image that will haunt your nightmares for the rest of your life.

5) Why weren't you invited?

Hey, what gives? Everyone is in on this sick fetish party, and they didn't invite you? Hard not to be hurt by that, eh?

MUSIC

Maniac 2000
MARK McCABE

WAS 'MANIAC 2000' A SECRET IRA ANTHEM ALL THIS TIME? YES, IT WAS

FOLLOWING a lengthy discussion with some people we met in the pub on Saturday night, WWN can exclusively confirm that the all-time classic floor-filler 'Maniac 2000' is in actual fact a coded message from the IRA, in a bid to convince young people to sign up and fight for a unified 32-county Ireland free from the shackles of occupation and oppression.

Released just three years after the Good Friday Agreement, 'Maniac 2000' was released when the Irish Republican Army had been engaged in a ceasefire and decommissioning

'Oggy, oggy, oggy, I. R. A.'

programme that many believed heralded a cessation of conflict in Ireland that would last forever… but as we continued to drink with our new-found theorists, the intrepid WWN team unlocked secret Republican messages that even DJ Mark McCabe may not have known were there.

Once we cracked that the 'sexy lady who had to get her thrill' was in fact a reference to Ireland herself, we quickly found parallels that suited our narrative. 'She was dressed to kill' is an obvious call for Ireland to rise up and kill British soldiers, and the 'mic in the left hand' is

clearly some sort of detonator, leaving the right hand free to 'bring this groove to you', or, bring the fight to mainland UK with a series of bombings aimed at crippling infrastructure and weakening the British resolve to continue their occupation of the North.

We attempted to contact Mark McCabe about the eerie parallels we had found in his song, but the DJ told us to 'Fuck away off and don't annoy him', which was all the proof we needed that we were right.

Whether or not the truth will ever be fully accepted, it's beyond clear to us that the popularity of the song in the summer months of 2000 are conclusive proof that the young people of Ireland truly recognised the subliminal messaging held within the track, and are fully ready to take arms against foreign invaders. As the song says: 'Oggy, oggy, oggy, I. R. A.'

Suburban Dictionary

'A bad dose' – phrase used to underplay the horrific pain a terminally ill person endured before passing away.

HEALTH

HOW TO AVOID SHAKING SOMEONE'S HAND AFTER THEY'VE COME BACK FROM THE TOILET

ARRIVED late to a social occasion or business function only to query where John, Eamon or Alan are, only to see them emerging from a nearby bathroom with a grin and an outstretched arm headed your way?

Shaking hands is a natural way to introduce yourself or reintroduce yourself for the 3,456th time to a friend or loved one, but if you are engaging in such a practice after someone is returning from a toilet it presents a germ-heavy nightmare.

Is it possible to avoid shaking their hand and not cause offence? Is there a more polite way to shy from the handshake than simply shouting, 'Get your hand away from me, which has just touched your willy or what have you. The state of you, you don't look the type to have the courtesy to wash your hands after, you knackbag'?

Thankfully WWN can confirm there is a solution.

1) Cut both your arms off

Once you have clocked the individual returning from the urinal has designs on shaking your hands, begin the process of fully dislodging your two arms and their attached shakeable hands from your body. Don't panic at the sight of the blood or the excruciating pain, bask in the knowledge that they can't rub their genital germs all over your hands any more.

2) There's more work to do

If you thought that's all there is to it, you're mistaken. There is nothing more rude and offensive than chopping your arms off to avoid a handshake, so while turning your back to the person briefly, attach state of the art animatronic robotic arms to your body, installing them at the bloody holes where your arms used to begin.

Turn swiftly back to the pissy-handed person in time to grip their hand with purpose with your robotic hands which look, feel and act just like real hands, and congratulate yourself on avoiding any awkward fallout from a less than ideal social situation.

3) Get yourself to a hospital

Seriously. You've lost a lot of blood there.

Suburban Dictionary

'Geebag' – an essential fashion item which can be used to place one's vagina inside of, for safe keeping.

WEDDINGS

FIVE THINGS ALL BEST MEN SHOULD PUT IN EVERY WEDDING SPEECH

HAS the honour of being best man at a friend's wedding been bestowed upon you? Then you better get a pen ready. This job is more than just organising a piss-up in Liverpool or a day of go-karting in the midlands somewhere. You need a speech, man!

Public speaking is nerve-wracking at the best of times, but when it's on the most important day of your best friend's life, you have to be sure to not put a single foot wrong. If you're caught for subject matter, then never fear: here's five things you must include, or the day is ruined. RUINED!

1) In-jokes

It's important that you pepper many vague references and in-jokes about your friendship with the groom throughout the speech. Whether there's ten guests or 200, they'll all love some baffling non-sequitur or half-story that goes nowhere, ending with the line, 'But sure I don't have to say any more about that.' You really, really do need to say more about it, but if you laugh enough at your own joke people will just assume it was funny and move on.

2) Curses

Just one 'fuck', just even one little 'shit', anything at all that you can let slip by accident in the middle of your speech so that the parents of the wedded couple can feel awkward while they glance over at the parish priest who swung a free dinner for himself. You don't have to be vulgar, but if you're in the middle of a story about some teacher you and the groom hated at school and you call him a 'miserable old cunt', well, so be it.

3) An elaborate slide-show/dance/flash mob

Look, do you want to feature on Joe.ie or not? This is your best pal's wedding. If your speech does not include a dance that you've been practicing for months, then hang your head in shame, you selfish prick.

4) A hostage situation

You've got the floor, you've got the mic. You've got a hundred unarmed guests. You could have anything you want, if you fire a gun in the air and tell everyone that none of them will see home again if the cops don't cooperate and give you your list of demands. Get someone released from jail. Get a fucking PlayStation!

5) Nudity

Hang your mickey out before you stand up. Just keep it out there through the whole speech. Say nothing, just read out the cards from people who couldn't be here today, with your penis resting on the table. See if anyone stops you, or points it out. Laugh it off if anyone gets offended. Jesus Christ, I thought this was a wedding. Relax, you fucking dry shites.

EXCLUSIVE

1) Yemen

War. Famine. Suffering. Yeah, not feeling so into chilling out in front of the TV tonight with this hanging over your head now, are ya? To think you were in a relatively chipper mood not 20 seconds ago.

2) Syria

Yup, kind of ruins that night out you had with friends filled with laughter. It's like, 'How can I laugh when this shit is going on?' We're not saying we agree with that sentiment, but Christ, just thinking about Syria now, it's like, fuck!

3) 700,000 people in Ireland live in poverty

So it's not technically an ongoing humanitarian crisis in the strictest sense of the phrase, which, when you

FOUR ONGOING HUMANITARIAN CRISES TO DEPRESS YOURSELF WITH

DO you find that you are just too content with your lot in life, and love nothing more than to enjoy your life and the friendships you have developed with those closest to you? Well then, you're going to love our list of four ongoing humanitarian disasters which will snap you right out of your good mood and guide you in the direction of feeling guilty for being afforded such a good life, comparatively speaking.

think of it, thank God it isn't, or else it would really ruin buying expensive clothes and stuff for us.

4) Venezuela

The socio-economic and political turmoil that has engulfed the Latin American country since the end of the Chavez reign has seen many people struggle with starvation and abject

poverty. The lingering thought of these people suffering would put a dent in any attempts to just simply enjoy your down time this weekend without being made to feel guilty.

BONUS HUMANITARIAN CRISIS: Shit, wait, how could we forget about Palestine, Palestine too, fuck that one is grim too. Enjoy your weekend!

HEALTH

'I JUST POP THE BAG RIGHT IN MY MOUTH, THEN POUR': WE TALK TO IRELAND'S TEA ADDICTS

'YOU think this is a fucking joke?' a garda screams in my face as I stifle some laughter, moments after he pulls over a dishevelled man who is found to have tea bags in his pockets along with a portable kettle.

'This shit ruins peoples' lives,' the garda I am shadowing for the day on the streets of Dublin tells me. I feel ashamed. I, like much of Ireland, have been in denial about our tea dependency.

Just last year, customs seized €300 million of Barry's Tea earmarked to be smuggled out of the country to emigrant tea addicts in Australia.

Time after time, Garda Ken, head of the Tactical Tea Unit (TTU), stops people on the street and searches them, and all the signs are there: pint of milk, portable kettle and a mug.

'Where ya going fella, huh? Off to find a tap or something is it, yeah?' Ken says as he pulls a man from the window of a house he was breaking into, all so he could hook his kettle up and drink down on the sweet addictive nectar of the gods we call tea.

It would be irresponsible of anyone to only show this side of tea addiction. The 'silent majority' of them often do this sort of thing in the comfort of their own home, often inviting others to join in. Come on, we all know one. You might be one. It's time Ireland woke up.

For research I attend a TA meeting. The sorry sight of people sharing their struggles while hovering by a table of biscuits and a keg of beer will stay with me forever. The devastation tea causes is real.

Next, Garda Ken guides me to what looks like a queue outside a cafe.

'They don't even hide their disease, the sad, pathetic bastards,' Ken remarks, clearly worn down from ten years on the TTU. 'We can't arrest them all, the country would grind to a halt.' Startling.

On Ken's suggestion, he tells me to engage with one of the addicts. I offer him a tea bag given to me by Ken. I'm unsure of the legal implications of all this, but I carry on.

'That's fucking piss. Is that what you think of me? You want me to drink piss?' an irate man, clearly 'teaking'

(when tea addicts are dying for their next fix), barks at me, and then for good measure mocks drinking urine from an imaginary air-penis.

'Well, you can piss off mate,' he adds, before reluctantly taking my one Lyons tea bag and placing it directly into his mouth, before reaching for a nearby kettle and pouring its contents down his throat. The combination would kill a non-addict, but not this weathered old tea pro.

A shocking episode. The addict was so desperate for a 'tit' (a tea hit) he was willing to drink Lyons instead of Barrys. There can be no greater illustration of just how out of control the tea problem is in Ireland. Before I know it, other tea drinkers surround me.

'We can't arrest them all, the country would grind to a halt'

'Any leaf?' 'Got some hot golden?' 'You carrying bag?' 'Is that China water?' I am overwhelmed by the ever-growing crowd; they maul at me, trying to locate any tea bag on my person.

'Hiss!' Rescuing me, Ken plugs in a kettle and sticks it on. It boils its unmistakable boil. Anticipating a tit, the addicts leave me and walk, zombie like, toward Ken, who reveals his garda badge. They disperse.

RELIGION

BEST COMMUNION BREAD IN IRELAND: A CHURCH-BY-CHURCH REVIEW

THE search for Ireland's best communion bread continues, with WWN's first installment for 2018 of this wildly popular series taking in the nation's capital, Dublin.

If you are not one of the 17 million people who have already read this series, you may not know that so far we've reviewed over 243 churches, and judged their communion bread on texture, design, taste and overall holiness.

A rating out of 5 stars is delivered, with 0 stars being 'a piss-poor excuse for the Body of Christ', with 5 stars being 'Yes, I can really taste Our Lord and Saviour Jesus Christ in this one'.

This week is the turn of Dublin suburb Dundrum and its recently refurbished church.

The newfangled facade is much admired, and is only a stone's throw away from Ireland's leading Cathedral of Capitalism, Dundrum Town Centre.

However, we're not here to judge architecture or the sort of sinful

shopping that will help secure your place in Hell. No, we're just here for the bread.

A kindly priest says mass and breaks the bread to a decent crowd of parishioners, which bodes well for the overall quality of the Eucharist.

We genuflect the living daylights out of the alter, as we do during every review, and all that's left to do is draw out our tongue and have a priest lash a bit of Body on it.

Texture: Not dry enough. Sad to say we don't even cough a little when placing the communion bread in the back our mouth. And there is little desire to reach for water to reinvigorate a palette starved of saliva.

Design: Nice to see some innovation here. The bread has an embossed scene of Jesus admonishing a woman for wearing an above-the-ankle skirt. The detail is impressive. Jesus's frown is very expressive.

Taste: Just the right side of bland with a hint of a metallic-like taste

which gives us plenty to think about while we are knelt down pretending to pray. Just what you want from a communion bread.

Overall Holiness: Ah yeah, it is Holy bread alright.

Final score: 3 out of 5 stars. Not a bad result as it places Dundrum Church's communion bread in the top 50. A result they can be proud of, but room for improvement.

Next week we stay in the capital and sample the communion bread from a pop-up church in Smithfield which is handed out from the back a HiAce van.

EDITOR'S NOTE: WWN formally apologises to the church we reviewed last week and ascribed a -4 star review, citing rude staff and an outright refusal by clergy to put the bread to our tongues. We now realise after some additional research that the Clonskeagh Mosque is in fact a mosque and not a church. Lesson learned.

Parish Notes

Pagan volunteers needed for Sunday's ritualistic burning of heathens. Good pay. May result in death by fire.

MOTORING

SIX THINGS YOU CAN DO WHILE STUCK ON THE M50

STUCK in a four-mile tailback on the M50 after someone accidentally turned on their indicator, sparking a butterfly effect on the several hundred cars in the driver's wake?

Although it is usually a cause for concern, WWN is here to suggest another alternative outlook on the following three hours you are sure to spend gridlocked in traffic.

Think of the possibilities that lie ahead of you: now is as good a time as any to do all the things you have been meaning to do in life.

1) Sign up to one of those online university courses

Look, you've a few hours to burn. Why not become a qualified psychologist or something? Even if you're not interested in marine biology, it'll pass the time.

2) Read *Ulysses*

Like everyone else you've pretended that you read the first couple of hundred pages before giving up because it's a load of old fanny, but now you can actually do that for real.

Hell, you might even have time to check a reading guide online so you know what the fuck Joyce was on about. Will trying to make sense of it make you go crazy? No more so than staring at a motionless '93 Nissan Micra that needs a good clean for seven hours will!

3) Do your taxes

Paying PRSI? Everything taken care of by your employer? Think again! You can claim money back on medical and dental expenses thanks to the Med 1 and Med 2 forms. Never been one for big intimidating forms? Don't fret, you've another two hours in traffic without moving an inch.

4) Knit a cardigan

What if your car battery packs it in? How will you keep warm as you wait for evening or morning traffic to not move at all? Oh, and before you knit that cardigan you can learn to actually knit! Finished already? Well, we're sure there are some chilly whales out there who would love to own the world's largest cardigan. Time is on your side.

5) Take up French again

God, you're always on about how you were dead good at in school and now you finally have the spare time to reacquaint yourself with the language of love.

6) Build an extra lane

Sick of going through this gridlock day in, day out, with no sign of improvement? Why not eat up some tarmac and get laying a new lane on the motorway to help you get from A to a shit load of traffic before getting to B some hours later.

DIET

HOW TO ALWAYS BE THE CO-WORKER WITH THE NICE LUNCH

Tired of being just another faceless employee cracking into a Tesco sandwich in the canteen of your already soul-kicking job? Wouldn't you rather be that one person in the office kitchen that rocks up with something absolutely incredible looking for lunch, the person who fills the whole office with the aroma of 'Yum, gimme some'? Well, if it's attention and a nice lunch you seek, we've got a few tips for you:

1) Bring in takeaway leftovers and heat them up

You don't have to bring in stunning looking leftovers, or indeed enough to constitute a whole meal. A little bit of reheated chicken curry goes a long way! All of your co-workers will immediately drop their gluten-free mediocrity and turn your way as you sit down at the table with a steaming plate of greasy leftovers. You don't even have to have takeaway the night before, you can honestly bring in half of a taco chips you found on the footpath and everyone will be like, 'Damn, you make that yourself?'

2) Get chips on a Monday

Chips are a great hump-day treat, or Friday blowoff before the weekend. At least one or more of your co-workers will arrive to the lunch table with a single and a cheeseburger during the week. Get your share of the attention pie by getting your chips on a Monday, right when everyone's in miserable form, still hungover, with nothing to eat except whatever misery wrap they've cobbled together. You can eat salad all week to make up for it. Chip Monday will see that you've got plenty of food kudos (fudos?) to see you through the next few days.

3) Eat a plate of dirt

Eating a plate of clay and worms may not seem appetising, but it'll make you the most interesting person at the table if you sell it right. Why are you eating dirt? Well, it's this great new diet you've heard of. One hundred per cent gluten-free, paleo, vegan, calorie-free dirt. Although people may be grossed out at first, soon they'll be licking their lips and wondering how they can get their hands on some dirt too. You've got them right where you want them: staring at you, paying you attention, giving you the little uptick in the middle of the day that you need to get you through the rest of this waking nightmare you call your career. Dig in! Savour it!

THIS IRISH COLLEGE STUDENT IS AUCTIONING OFF HIS VIRGINITY TO PAY FOR HIS STUDIES

AN Irish teenager is auctioning off his virginity in a bid to pay for his college studies and claims to have already received an offer of €23.19.

Fiachra Roche, 19, says he was offered the 'four-figure sum' after photographs of him circulated online, and that he is holding out for a more substantial offer before parting with his virginity.

'Some lad called John emailed me with the offer just a month after I originally posted the advert to my Facebook page,' Fiachra told WWN, who admitted to be still mulling over the fee. 'I'm gonna hold out for a little bit longer as my original intention was for a female to break me in, but look, I'm not fussy, just as long as I get enough to pay my college fees – I don't care if they're doing the sticking in or not.'

The Offaly man, who repeated his Leaving Certificate last year in order to get the 180 points needed for his forestry course in WIT, said he has been struggling to make ends meet, with books for college and soaring rent leaving him with very little expendable income to survive on.

'My parents' income was just over the threshold for me to get an education grant, so now I have to fork out three grand every year to study,' he explained. 'I suppose the problem is that my virginity can only be given away once, so I need to make it count financially for this to work.'

The full-time son of two revealed that he has kept the auction from his parents as he is scared the revelation would 'embarrass them'.

'I'm sure they won't hear about any of this despite the vast media attention I have received, and I'm confident that this whole thing will never come back to haunt me or affect my future prospects,' Fiachra concluded.

> **'I'm gonna hold out for a little bit longer as my original intention was for a female to break me in'**

RECIPE

REMEMBER THE 1.1 MILLION SOVIET SOLDIERS WHO DIED AT STALINGRAD WITH THIS DELICIOUS PANCAKE RECIPE

28 July 1942: Joseph Stalin issues 'Order No. 227', a military decision that declared that his forces would take 'not one more step back' from the advancing Nazi army that had swept east out of Germany into the heart of Russia. By August, the Germans had reached the city where the Red army were to make their finest, bloodiest stand. By February of the following year, over a million Russian troops would have given their lives, but their courage and fortitude would have ensured that the axis forces had been dealt one of the most crippling blows of the entire conflict, heralding the end of WWII itself. Now, who wants pancakes?

Ingredients
Flour
Eggs
Milk
Baking soda

This Pancake Tuesday, you don't have to stress and fuss over complicated gourmet recipes that require hours of prep – you can make simple, delicious pancakes that the whole family will love by following our simple recipe.

There are three main ingredients to pancakes: eggs, milk, and flour. We like to throw in a pinch of baking soda too, to help them rise; if you prefer a flatter, heavier pancake, then you can do without this. Now, just follow these simple steps.

Step 1
Just like the Russian forces who held off the advances of the Nazi forces, then considered the most unstoppable military force in the history of the world, making pancakes is all about proportions. We'll make it really simple, with our one-one-one rule. One cup of milk, one cup of flour, one egg. That's it. Stick with those proportions (throwing in one pinch of baking soda, if you like), and you literally cannot go wrong, unlike Hitler, who overestimated the abilities of his soldiers following relatively easy advances in Europe while deciding to advance into the icy climate of Russia.

Step 2
The battle of Stalingrad may have only lasted for six months, but the sheer scale of the carnage that raged non-stop throughout that time has left

it with the dubious honour of being one of the most bloody conflicts in the history of mankind. Losses on both sides piled up into ungodly numbers, with both armies sending wave after wave of young men to die in their droves. It was sheer numbers that swayed the battle in favour of the Reds, although not in terms of the number of soldiers that they had to fight. No, it was the sheer number of soldiers that they were prepared to lose that helped them win out over the thinly stretched Germans, the wave after wave of terrified young patriots that Russian generals allowed to pile up on the battlefield, stubbornly refusing to back down by even a single yard until victory was attained. With that in mind, mix the pancake ingredients with a whisk (or a fork, if you have no whisk) and allow the mixture to stand while you warm up your pan. You can use butter to oil up your pan and prevent the mixture from sticking, but a spray of Frylite offers a lower-calorie alternative.

Step 3
Pour a thin layer of mixture into the hot pan, and keep an eye out for the edges as these will be the first to rise, indicating that it may be time to flip the pancake. When you flip your pancake (and we recommend using a spatula. No showing off!), please remember that the second side will take a lot less time to cook than the first, so be vigilant or you will burn your pancake! Sometimes, we can't help but picture the faces of those poor, terrified soldiers, shipped in from all over Russia. For many, this was the first time they had ever left their native villages, to be brought with minimal training to a ruined city, have a rifle thrust in their hands and sent out to die in the bitter cold over a military decision they couldn't possibly have understood. Deserters were shot by the thousand. It was quite literally a hell on earth.

Step 4
Your pancakes are ready to go! Garnish with a condiment of your choice (we're partial to Nutella and bananas!)

HEALTH

REVEALED: THE LIST OF INJECTIONS YOU NEED BEFORE VISITING CORK

HEADING anywhere nice on holidays this year? No? Oh well, things could be worse, you could be heading to Cork. Oh, wait… we're sorry. You are going to Cork. Our sincere apologies. Well, to make it up to you, at least accept this list of important precautions you need to get before braving the Rebel county…

1) Vitamin D booster
Despite what you may have been told by Corkonians, the sun never shines in the south west. It's like that place in Iceland where it's night for a whole month each year, except it's just grey, and cold, and miserable. Despite this, there seems to be a high number of people wandering along the banks of the Lee with no tops on. That's the naturally occurring Vitamin D found in all Cork dwellers. You don't have it, so you need a top up before you go.

2) Dublin detoxification
Cork people can detect a Dub by smell alone, and will attack on sight. It's important that you remove all traces of Dublin from your person before crossing the demilitarised zone outside Fermoy. Scrub yourself down from top to toe with Dettol to rid yourself of the Dublin stench, and only wear clothes purchased in Cork branches of Penneys during your stay. This will involve walking naked into town so you can get to Penneys for

fresh clothes. Don't worry, nobody will notice.

3) Opinion suppressants
It is vital that you agree with Corkonians for the entire duration of your stay, especially when it comes to how class Cork is. You may at times find yourself wanting to say, 'Hold on, it's really not all that great here.' This is when your opinion suppressant pills will kick in, and stop you from saying

something you will later regret, such as, 'Fuck Cork', or 'Cork sucks'.

Enjoy your stay!

Health and Well-being Tip

99 per cent of health tips you read online are administered by someone who hasn't a fucking clue what they're talking about it.

CAN YOU BELIEVE IT TOOK EIGHT KIDS TO MAKE THIS PIECE OF SHIT SNOWMAN?

WWN will accept that the young children who took to People's Park in Waterford city to play in the snow yesterday may be too young to have any real experience in snow sculpture, but that fails to excuse the pathetic attempt at creating a snowman that can be seen at the north entrance to the park this morning.

Amazingly, eyewitnesses say that it took eight local kids almost the whole day to create the monstrosity, which currently stands slumped at a dismal five feet off the ground with a two-metre footprint, despite looking like someone just walked over to a pile of snow that the council had scraped off the footpath and stuck a carrot in it.

'It's a fucking waste of a dry scarf, so it is,' said one woman as she walked past, trying her best not to laugh at the dilapidated piece of shit snowman.

'If my kid made a snowman like that, I'd never let him outside of the house again,' said another, who brought his child to the park this morning specifically to point out the structural and aesthetic problems with what is rapidly becoming known as 'the shit snowman in the People's Park'.

Closer inspection of the supposed snowman reveals tell-tale signs of the difficulties the eight kids faced when creating the beast, which even upon completion could generously have been described as 'Jabba the Hutt-esque'. Speaking to an expert, WWN were able to trace the exact moment the children seem to have given up on creating a life-like representation of snowmen they had seen in cartoons or on TV and instead just said to themselves, 'Fuck it'.

'If my kid made a snowman like that, I'd never let him outside of the house again'

'So, these kids obviously didn't take into account that the snow currently covering the country is that horrible powdery "won't-pack" shit that is basically impossible to make a decent snowman with,' said Dr Victor Mandran, Waterford's foremost snow sculpture expert.

'You can see that they did their best to roll up a ball of snow for the base,

and that it basically crumbled away to nothing, leaving just a big pile of snow full of leaves and dogshit at the bottom. Then we can see where they tried to roll up another ball for the torso, not taking into account the sheer weight of a ball of snow that size. Did these dipshit kids think they could lift basically a cubic metre of water by themselves? You'd need a forklift for that. So, they just fucked it on top as best they could there. You can see salt tracks here and there, clearly from crying children who realised that they were failing harder than they'd ever failed before.

'Lastly, we come to the head, where nobody seems to have given even the slightest of fucks. A few rocks stuck here and there. A mitten, for some reason. A used condom, but that could have been thrown on it later. You'd forgive people for thinking this thing was just a rubbish bin that got caught in a snowdrift, in fairness. 1/10. Fucking useless.'

Kids across the country have been warned to 'try a bit harder' when creating snowmen during the rest of Storm Emma, with experts adding, 'If you don't know what you're doing, leave the snow for someone who does.'

CAN IRELAND SURVIVE WITHOUT BREAD? WE EAT OTHER FOOD TO FIND OUT

ONCE thought to be impossible, the unthinkable has occurred. Ireland, a country with supermarkets filled with a variety of food options, has run out of bread ahead of some snowfall.

Is the panic, violence and murder seen on the streets warranted? Is the sharing of the same gas memes by Irish media publications and websites still even a little bit amusing after they've beaten any fun out of the meme's lifeless corpse? There's no way to really know until they've posted another 7,892 of the things they've stolen from somewhere else.

In a bid to see if the nation of 4.5 million people could survive an occurrence such as a temporarily low supply of bread, WWN's crack team of science reporters and investigative journalists worked around the clock to find an answer.

Can Ireland survive without bread? We eat other food to find out, you fucking idiots.

Various canned foodstuffs:

Baked beans, chickpeas, spaghetti hoops. Tinned pineapples. Just a few of the foods on offer which have a shelf life of several years compared to the 'few days at best' that most bread is good for.

Could something other than bread help sustain us? Help us survive the snow?

It seemed at first we had made a grave fucking error as our entire staff is Irish, rendering our ability to think about stocking up and eating anything other than bread completely limited.

We pawed at the tins of food in a confused manner while some of us jumped up and down in an excited fashion shouting

'bread'. The labels on the outside of the tins suggested the contents had some nutritional value, but how can anyone trust anything other than bread?

Tin opener:

After extensive research on the internet, we discovered a magical tool which must have been moulded from some sort of witch spell. Named 'tin opener', we examined it for hours but could not use it to coax the food from the tins.

Pointing at the tin opener while shouting, 'Leave food! I demand you to transport yourself to my mouth,' proved pointless.

I'm hungry:

Without bread, the giver of all life, we grew restless, tired and hungry. One staff member, hallucinating, mistook a colleague for a piece of bread and tried to force them into a toaster. The struggle lasted all of ten minutes before others thankfully intervened and helped to place our colleague, who resisted and screamed, into the toaster.

Flesh:

Flesh is not bread. But flesh is food. Flesh feeds us. We are no longer hungry. The snow cannot hurt us anymore.

But bread?

Yes, bread. I curse the bastard editor who sent us on this suicide mission. It was insanity to think we could survive this sort of weather without a vast supply of bread. Oh, God, I'll never see my children again. I've never died of bread withdrawal before. Is it painful? Maybe I will do the unimaginable before I get the dreaded 'bread brain' and go mad. Wait, is that … Oh, thank God, it's a human-sized sliced pan. Now, if I can force it into the toaster I might live beyond today.

'THAT WEATHER WILL KILL OFF ALL THE OLD FLU BUGS,' INSISTS LOCAL MOTHER

A COUNTY Waterford mother has insisted that Ireland's latest cold snap will kill off all of the latest bouts of influenza, despite having no medical training or background, WWN can confirm.

Peggy Roche, who made the statement to her sons and daughters yesterday afternoon, believed the wind chill factor mixed with the snow is nature's way of getting rid of one of the worst bouts of flu the country has seen in years,

which has already claimed over 100 lives.

'I knew the minute I heard about the Australian flu that nature would take care of it herself,' Mrs Roche explained, who has been an assistant shopkeeper for 30 years.

Despite no medical evidence to suggest that

snow somehow kills influenza, and the fact that low temperatures actually increase its rate of survival in the air, Peggy persisted with her theory.

'No better time for it now,' she went on. ''Twas an awful dose all the same. Mary Holden down the street

was in the hospital for eight weeks with it sure – the priest and everything was called. Luckily she pulled through in the end. Must have been the cold weather.

'Watch now, wait 'till you see. Everyone will be as right as rain after this passes,' she concluded.

MET ÉIREANN CONFIRM CURRENT FOG IS 90 PER CENT VAPE

A SPOKESPERSON for the Met Office has confirmed that the dense fog currently coating the country is a result of high amounts of vape smoke, probably due to New Year's smoking resolutions.

Currently at an orange warning level, the country is experiencing thick clouds of mist reducing visibility significantly on all major routes, which meteorologists are estimating is about 90 per cent e-cigarette smoke, with the remaining 10 per cent consisting of regular, good old-fashioned tobacco.

Experts expect the poor visibility to last well into February, when the resolve of people attempting to quit smoking starts to wane and they go back on the fags.

'Yeah, it's all these people who got the space harmonica for Christmas,' said a spokesperson for Met Éireann, referring to the oversized vape pipes that have replaced the slender pens that people used to use.

'I remember when e-cigs looked like fake cigarettes, but now they look like a lightsaber fucked a clarinet, and produce more vapour than the Poolbeg incinerator. With hundreds of thousands of smokers looking to give up smoking in favour of smoking something else, it was inevitable that you get this kind of fog in the country. But don't worry, it's perfectly harmless, or so they tell us.'

The find was made after several people noticed that the fog was not odourless like regular mist, but instead carried a sickly sweet tang of marshmallows or bubblegum, leaving the entirety of the eastern seaboard smelling like a Yankee Candle.

MOVING SCENES AS PUBLIC REUNITED WITH THEIR LOCAL PUB AFTER STORM EMMA

IT was the moment they feared would never come again, but despite the paralysing horror at the thought that they would never see the inside of their local pub again, many members of the public have been reunited with their beloved watering holes after the worst of Storm Emma dissipated.

Hugging the walls of pubs around the country, tightly gripping their facades while delicately whispering 'I love you' and 'I'll never leave you again', thousands of regulars eased their way into their dearest pubs relieved the nightmare is now over.

Camera crews around the country caught the heartwarming moments pub attendees rushed from their cars, racing towards their locals like it was their love interest and they were Hugh Grant in an average rom-com movie currently streaming on Netflix.

'It's been a confusing, scary and vulnerable time for me,' remarked one local pub attender to WWN. 'You think maybe that's it, you'll never see them again. I cried. I rang the barman constantly. I cried some more. It's been a heartbreaking 36-hour separation.'

Erotically caressing the fixtures and fittings of their local, the public teared up as it caught site of the old bodhran that sits above the bar only to break down completely when trying to order a pint of Guinness.

'You never think of weather as pure evil until it causes a separation like this, but what that snow did to us… I'll never forgive it,' explained another local, who hadn't felt this abandoned since his father left to go to his local 46 years ago, only to never be heard of again.

PANIC SHOPPERS PURCHASE LAST REMAINING SUPERMARKET AHEAD OF STORM EMMA

CUSTOMERS looking for their favourite supermarkets were left stranded this morning following a large-scale panic-buy ahead of Storm Emma, WWN can reveal.

Shoppers up and down the country arrived at supermarket locations to find bare foundations, with fire crews and emergency water teams desperately

working around the clock to stop leaks from gas and water pipes after the stores were literally ripped from the ground by buyers.

'Ah, its a fucking mess,' one Waterford councillor told WWN. 'There's nowhere to get naughtin' now, and for what? A few days of snow?'

Ireland's last remaining Aldi store was purchased in Mitchelstown in County

Cork at 8:59 p.m. last night, leaving the country now supermarket-less for the foreseeable future.

'Snow can be boiled to make drinkable water,' said one maniacal-looking man we spoke to, who was desperately clawing the earth where Tramore's Tesco store was once located.

Gardaí are warning shoppers of 'fake

supermarkets' being sold across the country, the majority of which are run by opportunistic crime gangs.

'We've had several instances where people bought what they believed were supermarkets, but when they arrived home, they were found to be local convenience stores, with one woman conned into buying a Daybreak store that had several years of back taxes to be paid, leaving her with a large bill,' a garda statement read, before advising people to 'best stick to known-brand stores'.

'SURE isn't it probably their first time ever seeing snow, let alone playing in it?' marvelled Waterford woman Ciara Shandling, looking out her front window at the Middle Eastern kids from seven doors down playing in the deluge of snow dumped on the country by Storm Emma overnight.

'THAT MUST BE NICE FOR THEM,' SAYS LOCAL WOMAN WATCHING MUSLIM KIDS PLAY IN SNOW

'Look at them, they probably haven't a clue

what's going on. There's never snow out there where they come from, wherever that is. Syria, or one of those places you see on the news.'

Shandling (45) noticed the family of five kids out playing in the snow this morning, along with around 100 white children, about whom who she passed no remarks. Taking note of the Middle Eastern children's preparedness for the cold weather, Shandling has surmised that generous government aid has helped the probably refugee family to enjoy the winter fun.

'And look at them there, all dressed up for the winter with their hats and coats and scarves and gloves, never mind them,' continued Shandling, who has closely monitored the family's every movement

every day since they moved into the neighbourhood two years ago.

'All of that would cost a fair bit, and I wonder where they'd be getting the money for that? The father works somewhere alright – I see him going off in the morning – but the mother doesn't go anywhere. Probably not allowed work, isn't that the way with a lot of them? Still, five kids all dressed up in the best winter gear. I think you know who's paying for that, don't you? You and me, that's who.'

Meanwhile, WWN have caught up with the Zaharrla family as they played on the green, with Limerick-born dad Dr Ahran Zaharrla confirming that this is indeed his family's first time seeing snow since their skiing trip to Andorra last year.

THIS GRANDAD WAS ABANDONED ON THE SIDE OF THE ROAD AFTER HIS FAMILY SAID HE WASN'T CUTE ENOUGH ANYMORE

PEOPLE online have reacted with shock and outrage at the story of 89-year-old Jeremiah Pearson who was abandoned by his daughter, son-in-law and their children after they concluded he was no longer the sort of old person often found in inspirational posts and videos on the internet and on app feeds, WWN has learned.

No longer possessing the quality associated with a kindly and adorable older person, Pearson's value to his family when it came to helping his children and grandchildren obtain likes and video views online had become greatly diminished.

'We're talking about someone who was the wrong sort of old, not the old videos viewers find adorable. He wasn't visiting the grave of his wife everyday with fresh flowers, that kind of shit people love. He was just getting old and not in a cute way. So what are we supposed to do? Feed and clothe him? Even though he's getting us no

> ## 'We're talking about someone who was the wrong sort of old, not the old videos viewers find adorable'

viral videos and photos. He's not even a meme for Christ sake,' explained his son-in-law Josh Coltrane.

'I'm not being bad or anything, but it's been a long time since any of my friends went crazy for any Insta or Snapchat stories about him. He was boring old, it's best for everyone he left, ya know?' Pearson's youngest grandchild, 14-year-old Esme Coltrane shared with WWN.

A legion of Twitter users reacted angrily to images of Pearson on the side of a road circulating online, with some labelling what his family did as 'inhuman', 'disgraceful' and 'evil', failing to accept the reality of

how useless old people can be when they're not being exploited for cheap likes on the internet.

Pearson himself is believed to be too upset to address journalists who have requested an interview for a news piece they hoped would go viral if it had the required uplifting ending.

Ironically, news that he had been left on the side of the road discarded provided Pearson's family with the viral hit they craved as people shared the story far and wide.

'Okay, we'd reconsider what we've done and we think Grandpa can come home. Maybe we could mark it with a video where we all hug, you know, one of those heartwarming ones,' offered his daughter, Vanessa.

Did You Know?

You're going to hate the next government, and the government after that, and the government after that, and...

TRAVEL

TRAVEL! Do it when you're young, when you have the drive and energy to get from country to country and really get the best of the experiences that await you! Of course, this leaves you at a disadvantage when it comes to funding, but do you really want to wait until you're old and slow to have saved up enough cash before you get out there and see what the world has to offer? Or do you want a cheap and easy option?

It's an easy one to answer, and we might have something you'll be interested in. FREE accommodation in Colombia, one of South America's most South American countries. We'll even swing you a free flight! Sound interesting? Here's all you need to do.

1) Get a passport
Uh, check! Of course you have a passport! You wouldn't be travelling without a passport! If you have a passport, we have a ticket with your name on it. Head to the airport and away you go! Want a few drinks in the airport bar? It's all on us!

TRY THIS EASY TRICK TO GET FREE ACCOMMODATION IN SOUTH AMERICA

2) Get to this address
That's our friend in Colombia, he's a real nice guy. You can stay in his place, free of charge! He'll take you out to a few hotspots, and keep your wallet in your pocket, it's all on us! Enjoy the sights, sounds and spectacle of this fantastic country, and stay there until we tell you it's time to come home!

3) Put all of this cocaine up your bumhole
Did you enjoy your trip? Yeah? Great! It's good to have some stories to tell. Now check out this photo we've just sent you. That's your mam and dad's house, isn't it? Well, it has a pretty

high chance of not getting burned to the ground if you just fill your colon with as many condoms full of pure cocaine as you can, and get it back to us in the next 48 hours. Otherwise, this lonely planet might get that little bit lonelier for you! Hurry back, we're sending you to Afghanistan next!

Suburban Dictionary

'A cúpla focal' – Irish for 'a cup of fuck all', used by non-Irish speakers when explaining the level of their Irish speaking skills.

EMPLOYMENT

POLISH LADS: A PERFORMANCE REVIEW

HI, take a seat. So, you Eastern European tradesmen have been working in the country for a generation or so, and you all seem perfectly okay with how we refer to you all as 'Polish' rather than the nationality you actually are. It's just so hard for us Irish people to take the time to differentiate between Latvian and Estonian people, so thanks for meeting us in the middle on that one. Okay, just a few points with today's review, nothing to worry about. Let's begin:

1) Punctuality

First of all, I just want to say that there's nobody upset at you, okay. You're doing nothing wrong here. But there have been numerous instances when you all have shown up to do whatever painting, carpentry, plumbing or tiling that you've been contracted to do, at the exact time that you've said you would arrive.

Look, we know that's the way you're used to doing things back in Poland or wherever, but in Ireland if a tradesman says he's going to come on Monday at 11 a.m., he really means that he might come on Thursday at 8 p.m.. You guys seem to arrive at the time that you've agreed with the customer, and that seems to be confusing a lot of Irish people. Again, we're not angry, but it's something that you might need to keep in mind in future.

2) Communication

Guys, we'd just like to say that it's great how you lads work in pairs, really. And the way that you all seem to have paired up so that one of you has perfect English while the other one doesn't seem to speak a single word is really quite unique.

Customers are really happy with how they can line out exactly how you should go about your job by speaking to you like you're a fucking idiot, while you simply smile and say that it's 'no problem', before turning to your non-English speaking pal and convey the nine minutes of what they just yammered on about with two lines of Polish. Keep it up.

3) Equipment

Lads? Having all the equipment and materials needed to complete a job before you arrive? Loving it. But if we're being critical, and that's really our job here, to create helpful criticism, it's maybe a little bit unfair to those tradesmen who prefer to opt for an approach where they show up, look around, head out to 'get stuff' and then disappear for a month. Maybe just try to see things from their point of view for a while.

Summary

Okay, so overall, very pleased with your work. If you were to take anything from this review, please just try to see it from the point of view of tradesmen who have been in the country a lot longer than you have. Those that have worked for years to create an environment where they can charge whatever they like, work whenever it suits them, and really just do whatever they want.

When you came over here first you weren't much of a threat to them, thanks to our country's natural xenophobia, but ten years down the line all that has been forgotten thanks to your work ethic and craftsmanship. But still, leave something for the rest of the team, okay? Blame some of your poor workmanship on someone else every now and then, overcharge a few elderly people, that kind of thing. Let's keep the playing field a bit fair, okay?

SAFETY

SOME IMPORTANT FACTS ABOUT CARBON MONOXIDE

SAFETY

HI there! We notice that you're still reading, probably just your eyes involuntarily drifting down from that young woman's wonderful figure there. Well, if you've followed us this far, then please allow us to take a moment to talk to you about carbon monoxide, the silent killer that could… Okay, come back from the boobie pic there, just for a second.

1) CO is odourless, tasteless and invisible.

Don't tell yourself that you'll 'smell a carbon monoxide leak' in your house. You won't. You won't know you're being poisoned until it happens, and by then it might be too late. Sorry to trick you into reading this article by using boobs, but we really needed to get your attention in some way, and attention spans these days don't last long unless they're accompanied by sexy imagery.

2) You need an alarm

See that girl there? Wow, she's pretty, right? Now imagine she came into your house one night, up the stairs,

Wonderful World of Science

Micra biologists have confirmed for the first time that Nissan Micras and biology may be better studied separately.

while you were sleeping, into the bed beside you, and then stuffed your throat with cotton wool until you asphyxiated and died. That's carbon monoxide! The woman is carbon monoxide! Now wouldn't you want an alarm in your house to stop that from happening? You would! Of course you would! So get one, and check it regularly.

3) Have gas boilers and solid fuel stoves serviced regularly

If you want to keep seeing sexy images of scantily clad girls in tabloid newspapers and clickbait-heavy websites, then for the love of Christ service your boilers and stoves on a regular basis. Now please, read this all again and concentrate this time! Your life 100 per cent depends on it!

RELIGION

FIVE PLACES TO HAVE A SNEAKY PRAY

Parish Notes

The parish is in mourning after fatal organ failure means choir will be backed by Casio keyboard for foreseeable future.

WITH the liberals and their Catholic-bashing mantra slowly making it increasingly difficult for followers to express their beliefs in public life, a large majority of worshipers are now being forced underground to pray to the Almighty Father.

But just where are the best places to partake in a sneaky pray? We've asked five staunch Catholics about their favourite places to pray while out and about.

John, 47, secondary school teacher
'Whenever I get the urge, I break the glass button in the hall and trigger the fire alarm so the whole school has to evacuate. The kids always get the blame, but I find this is the perfect time to take my shirt off and whip my back repeatedly with my beads while reciting at least one decade of the Rosary. I find the PE hall to be an ideal location to pray, due to the acoustics and its varnished wooden floor which is perfect for wiping up any blood splatters.'

Mary, 39, shop assistant
'I have a statue of the Blessed Virgin hidden behind the Cornflakes section which faces down aisle 3, so every time I'm kneeling down to pack the shelves, I sneak in a little prayer. The boss just thinks I'm working.'

Jacob, 14, junior cert student
'Every Thursday morning me and two other classmates mitch off Tech Drawing and go down the back lane for a quickie. One lad keeps watch while the other two pray. I could get in anywhere between three or four prayers in one sitting. I'm trying to cut down, but it's just too nice.'

Martina, 43, customer care representative
'I put people on hold and tell them I need to speak to the supervisor about their account, but it's not the supervisor they think, it's God, and he usually tells me to hang up on them and go out for a smoke. God's funny like that.'

Beatrice, 32, housewife
'When I'm caught short, I find the nearest bar or restaurant and ask them if I can use their toilets. Nine times out of ten it's a prayer to Saint Anthony to help me find something, but sometimes I just like to have a spontaneous pray about whatever. I must have God driven mad with all my zany thoughts.'

Fr Niall O'Higgins, 39, priest
'I drive from my parish in Louth down to Kerry every morning at 5 a.m. Then I swim out to a boat I have moored two kilometres off the coast there. Then I row for about three hours, and when I'm nice and alone in the middle of the Atlantic Ocean I hammer the life out of an 'Our Father'. But I always feel like someone, something, is still watching me.'